Correction: Two names in this copy, Barbara Germait and Julie Rudig. should read Barbara Germiat and Jacqueline Rudig. WWA journal staff sincerely apologizes for these errors. All future copies will show the correct names.

Creative Wisconsin Literary Journal
A Collective Work

Copyright © 2017 WWA Press, Wisconsin Writers Association
Copyright © 2017 for individual pieces within this publication belongs to contributors named, whose works are reproduced herein with their permission.

All rights reserved.
Creative Wisconsin is produced and published by the Wisconsin Writers Association, Incorporated, a registered 501(c)(3) nonprofit corporation in the State of Wisconsin.

# A Tribute to Libbie Faulkner Nolan

Elizabeth "Libbie" Faulkner Nolan, artist and writer, is a lifetime member of WWA who celebrated her 100$^{th}$ birthday in January 2017. And she's still writing. Libbie recalls working with Robert Gard, when WWA was in its formative years as the Wisconsin Rural Writers Association (WRWA). But she is best known for the drawings of country mailboxes that graced the covers of WRWA newsletters from 1962 to 1994. This edition of the Creative Wisconsin Literary Journal is dedicated to this prolific artist and writer who contributed so many years of wonderful talents to the Wisconsin Writers Association. A short story by Libbie is the first selection in this year's Creative Wisconsin Literary Journal.

# Acknowledgments

The Creative Wisconsin Literary Journal proudly features selected works written by members of the Wisconsin Writers Association.

WWA sincerely thanks all members who contributed prose and poetry entries, and regrets that all entries could not be included. WWA also thanks the volunteer members who worked to put this book together, including the prose and poetry selection committees, Diana Schramer, who edited this issue, Nicolette Pierce, who facilitated page layout and readied the book for publishing, and Laurel Bragstad, journal coordinator.

Of course, none of this work would be possible without the ongoing support of the entire WWA membership.

Thank you.

# Creative Wisconsin Literary Journal

## Wisconsin Writers Association
## October, 2017

# Table of Contents

**Lexington and Beyond: Our American Revoluntionary War,** Elizabeth "Libbie" Faulkner Nolan ............................. 1

**A Place Just Right,** Maryclaire Torinus ..................... 3

**Crossroads,** Julie Rudig ................................................ 9

**Is That You, Miss C?** Virginia Read ........................ 15

**Stealth Love,** Lora Hyler ........................................... 21

**The Existential Poet,** Sara Burr ................................ 27

**Between Then and Now,** Sara Sarna ........................ 28

**Legacy,** Joanne Nelson ............................................. 30

**Portrait of David Forsyth,** Barbara Germait ............ 32

**Racing into Rain: A Midwestern Metaphor,** Mike Orlock ................................................................. 34

**My Grandma's Orange,** Chris Roerden ................... 36

**Covenant,** Nancy Bauer-King ................................... 40

**On Their Own Terms,** Nancy Jesse ........................ 44

**Riding the Number 19 Bus,** Nancy Rafal ................ 49

**Fears? Not!** Greg Peck ............................................. 50

**The Girls with the Grandmother Faces,** Marjorie Pagel ............................................................. 52

**The Light,** Shirley Barker ......................................... 54

**Peacemaker,** Raymond Schrab .................................. 56

**Hiraeth,** Dan Kussart ................................................ 62

**Wash. Dry. Fold. Repeat—Sailor Style,**
Julia McCurdy Gimbel ................................................. 68
**Big D, Little D,** Mel Miskimen ................................. 74
**At Last,** John Leighton ............................................. 80
**Trading Up,** Liz Rhodebeck ...................................... 82
**Vapor Trail,** Diana Randolph .................................... 84
**Lost in her Square,** Bev Larsen ................................ 86
**She's Gone (1974)** Dan Meyer ................................. 88
**The Poet,** Evan Sasman ............................................ 90
**The Road to Nowhere,** Jane Yunker ........................ 91
**Anything,** Eric Montag ............................................. 94
**Critique Chic,** Joel Habush ..................................... 100
**A friend speaks of her dying father,** Lisa Rivero .. 106
**The Defibrillator Meal,** Ed Sarna .......................... 107
**Sister Abagail's Snow Socks,**
Thomas Wayne King ................................................. 111
**When Madness Took Over the Milwaukee Repertory Theater,** Ludmilla Bollow ..................... 117
**Whenever Women Have Lived,** Lisa Rivero ......... 123
**Music and the Man,** Susan Hunnicutt .................... 126
**On Valentine's Eve,** Lisa Vihos .............................. 128
**Friendship by the Slice,** Nancy Runner ................. 129

*The 2017 edition of Creative Wisconsin Literary Journal is dedicated to Libbie Nolan. The short piece below is excerpted from her article that appeared in the Autumn 2014 edition of Landmark, published by the Waukesha County Historical Society & Museum, Inc.*

## Lexington and Beyond: Our American Revolutionary War

Elizabeth "Libbie" Faulkner Nolan
*100 years young in 2017*
WWA Lifetime Member
Big Bend, WI

It was on April 19, 1775, that the first battle of our country's Revolutionary War was fought at Lexington, Massachusetts. A year later, July 4, 1776, our Declaration of Independence was signed, thus declaring our collective colonies to be a free, independent country.

Two centuries later—would you believe?—two friends who have lived in the little Midwestern village if Mukwonago, Wisconsin would discover an unusual and strange coincidence. They found that they were both descendants of two of those militiamen who fought in that Lexington skirmish.

Bob Figie, who had seen the National Society of Daughters of the American Revolution insignia on my door, said he also had an ancestor who fought in the Revolutionary War and brought me a copy of his family records.

Imagine our surprise to read that his ancestor had also fought in the Battle of Lexington and had come from the state of Connecticut. Bob's ancestor, Roswell Graves, was born in 1740 in Haddam, Conn. My ancestor, Gideon King, was born in 1747 in Suffield Conn.

My family records also indicate that Samuel Butler, the grandfather of my great-great-grandmother, Lydia Butler Moore Cheney had fought in the Battle of Yorktown where Lord Cornwallis surrendered to General George Washington, thus ending the Revolutionary War.

An unusual bit of history: here is a family that has an ancestor who fought in the first battle and another who fought in the last battle of the Revolutionary War that created a free and God loving country in this world.

# A Place Just Right

Maryclaire Torinus
Brookfield, WI

She is restless today. As we look out across the golden meadow, cuddling amidst tangled sheets, my chin rests upon wisps of her silky hair. I point to the field swallow standing guard over her young brood. Mom whistles their song. Even now, she can mimic any birdcall. I smile at her melodic trill; still, tears tremble and leak beneath my lashes. A sob catches in my throat threatening the tranquility, so I try to smother the panic impatient to erupt. I don't want to frighten her; we are on a holy mission.

With feeble effort, she tries to tighten my already-firm grip around her. For months, she shuffled with fallen arches and stooped shoulders, bony bunions rubbing raw the edges of her woolen slippers—slippers so tattered they barely contained her nylon-enshrouded feet. Now, dementia devastates her brain and cancer ravages the one drooping breast and beyond. But in my mind, she stands as stately as the silver birch that shades the woodland stream.

As the hours wear on, her breathing becomes labored. I imagine her soul, full term, yearning for freedom from its earthly womb. Antsy. With a looming instinct that the confining space was only meant to be temporary, that a mysterious, magnificent world lies within reach. She stirs beneath my protection. "What would I have done without you?" These are the last words I will hear from her.

The birthing of her soul has commenced, and my inclination to press her close is no match for its muscular resolve to be released. It would be easy for me to remain as I am—hovering and doting—but mothers don't surrender easily with a child clinging to their hip. So my role as daughter transitions to that of midwife. I change tactics, try to relax my grip, and quietly sing the lullaby she once sang to me: "Tis the gift to be simple, tis the gift to be free, tis the gift to come down where you ought to be, and when you find yourself in the place just right—you'll be in the valley of love and delight." My voice falters.

I gently pry her from me and position a pillow beneath her head. Settling into a chair, the hours of dusk disappear, holding her hand. As sunlight wanes and shadows dance across the floor, strains of Schubert alight. The room fills with the fragrance of lavender as I anoint her hands and feet. Prayerfully, I nudge her toward the "valley," fertile with purple petunias, singing and skating (her favorite pastimes), and brimming with happiness and wholeness.

My eighty-year-old mother has become unresponsive, but the staff asserts she can hear me. "I love you, Mom," I announce with conviction, testing their assumption. Her eyelids quiver.

Midnight passes, and the nursing schedule shifts as concerned faces come and go with morphine in hand. Standing to stretch, I cross the room to take in Mom's view. Shards of starlight grace the garden: a labyrinth of sleepy flowers and boxy hedge where lightning bugs dart and flash . . . where chalky white angelic sculptures and stone benches glow in ghostly repose.

I turn to concentrate on her wedding portrait that my father placed on the table. I puzzle at his choice. Maybe he wanted to focus on the memories of her as a twenty-four-year-old as he finds himself bracketed between two frames of reality: the weddedness of their youth and the unrecognizable form lying before me. How does the "then" and "now" merge so swiftly?

The colorless photo features her dark, shoulder-length curls framed by a modest chiffon veil secured to a halo of lilies of the valley. I look nothing like her. She is olive-skinned and French; I am blonde, fair, and Norwegian.

While I resemble my father, a great deal about my mother is me.

The night lingers. I fill its solitude with the flickering of candlelight and the monotonous recitation of a rosary. The accumulation of hours sitting sentry propels miles of memories forward until, nearly spent, they dribble to nothing. And then, we are here, left to this room. Suddenly, loneliness and exhaustion are evident as the painful truth settles in: our memory making is finished.

Searching the shadowy space, I wonder if ancestors are present waiting to escort Mom home. I fantasize that her four sisters, my favorite aunts, are bobbing, clucking, and fussing over us like a clutch of chubby hens. This comforting reverie is an unexpected respite and causes me to lose track of Mom's decline.

For the last six hours, her breathing would cease for forty-five seconds at a time. I'd think it finished, only to see her snatch erratic gulps of stale air to prolong the vigil. So I begin the tedious count once again, and by the time I reach fifty, my heart is pounding.

I wait. But this time she does not struggle to inhale. Finding no pulse, my hands begin to shake. I stand to pace . . . *I still need her . . . I'm not ready . . . I thought I could be.* "Mom, don't leave me," I cry into the night. Daring to turn and confront fate, I recognize that my bird whistler is no longer here. She lies pale and still.

Wracking sobs take hold, and a torrent of tears can no longer be restrained. *A good mother should never die.* I try to convince myself that she hasn't—she simply waits for us, just beyond my vision.

Eventually, with the outpouring of anguish, a calm washes over the room. I sense the crowning of her soul. It is palpable. Lilies and kindness, lilacs and grace bursting forth from every pore. Her labor, concluded. Her face, peaceful and proud. Triumphant even. I place a kiss upon her familiar cheek. Gathering her to myself, I memorize her smell . . . rose-scented shampoo, minted breath, salt, and musk. Her final essence my new cologne.

I gently lay her down and pull the knobby afghan firm to her chin, tucking it in tight as if bolting a door against the chill and stiffness of an approaching winter.

I desperately try to preserve her before the searing flames of cremation consume the arms that held me and that I held onto.

As I glance out onto the lawn, I notice the emerging dawn has announced itself with a rosy hue. On this fresh morn, she does not rise with the lark. I should call Dad, but I want her to myself for a few moments longer. It is selfish, I know, but she was my mother, my sister, my friend. Grabbing my makeup bag, I reapply my ruby-shaded lipstick and place one last kiss before I leave. There, for all to witness, the mark of affection emblazoned on her forehead—like the Hindu bindi, the feminine embellishment to signify achieving one's earthly purpose.

I leave the building for the last time and stumble into my life without her, deeply inhaling the frosty, crisp air of autumn. Suddenly, a burst of energy rushes through me, and I shiver at Mom's glancing caress. I feel her soul take flight, effortless, yet mighty. On course and confident. To a place just right.

I gaze into the meadow—and there, birds gather and flitter and sing. And from somewhere, I hear her mimic their song.

# Crossroads

Julie Rudig
Wauwatosa, WI

"Well, Mom, how do you like it?" Julie said, twirling into my bedroom, store tags flying and face aglow. Her pirouette landed right next to my bed where I sat cross-legged, savoring the Sunday newspaper. I looked up, and there stood my fifteen-year-old daughter modeling a brand-new denim miniskirt remarkably reminiscent of one I'd worn decades before.

Julie and her friend Andrea had walked to the mall that autumn afternoon, and Julie had taken the birthday money from her grandma along with her. Still, it never dawned on me they might deviate from their usual socializing and Sephora sampling to actually go shopping.

Perhaps interpreting my silence as disapproval, Julie quickly began to justify her purchase by reciting Principle Number Two of the Four Principles of

Shopping she had learned so diligently under my wing. "It goes with just about everything," she announced in a voice so like my own.

I kept silent and leaned forward for a better look at this first-of-its-kind purchase. I couldn't help but notice her left knee still bandaged from her latest attempt to turn a single cartwheel into a double.

Both hands now firmly planted on her hips, Julie cautiously advanced to Principle Number Three. "It will never go out of style," she said.

Breaking my silence, I challenged her to recall the all-important Principle Number One. "But was it on sale?" I asked. Our eyes met, and the world as we had known it stood still.

Determined and unflappable, Julie quickly yanked off the dangling price tag and stuffed it in the pocket of her new Gap miniskirt. Clearly, nothing I might say would separate her from this proud moment or that overpriced skirt.

"No, Mom, it was not on sale," she readily admitted as she narrowed her mascara-laden, purple-shadowed eyes, evidence that a stop at Sephora had indeed been part of their day. Courageously, she proceeded to invoke our well-worn Principle Number

Four. "But I just had to have it!" Julie laughed. We both laughed.

The previous year had been filled with many rites of passages for Julie, my firstborn and only daughter. Eighth-grade graduation, first summer job, and freshman dance had all been milestones in her life and consequently in mine. Yet in this moment nothing seemed more life-changing than her shattering of the exclusive ritual we had practiced since she was born: Julie had gone shopping with her own friend, with her own money, and without me!

As if her glaring pride in that accomplishment wasn't enough to unsettle me, I found myself struggling with how to tell her the skirt clung too close and hung too short. As I searched for the right words, I recalled the memory of another skirt and another time.

I was Julie's age when I borrowed my friend Nancy's denim miniskirt. Sharing favorite possessions was a way Nancy and I validated our friendship, not unlike what Julie and Andrea do today. Secrecy was essential, especially because my mother frowned on borrowing or lending anything to anyone. Besides, Nancy outfits were typically a size or two smaller than mine.

Our secret swaps were convenient because our families were next-door neighbors. Nancy and I would meet after supper in the nineteenth-century red-brick alley that ran behind our houses. With an endless supply of kids, the alley served as a neighborhood playground. Waiting until after the younger kids went home to bed allowed us private time to trade clothes, books, dreams, and secrets. We'd sit Indian-style on the red clay bricks, "fire bricks," we called them because they held the warmth of the afternoon sun long after sunset. Together we'd listen for the nine clangs of St. Leo's church bells that signaled our common curfew.

The morning I borrowed Nancy's skirt, I dawdled until Mom left for work before I put it on and headed for school. As I waited at my usual bus stop, feeling prettier than I knew I ought to, I had my first experience as the object of a man's admiring gaze. My heart raced as a vague, warm sensation coursed through my body. I dared not move any part of me except my eyes, which darted this way and that, trying to determine—to confirm—that it was indeed I who was worthy of this grown man's attention. The casual yet deliberate glance came from a truck driver about the age of my father, who had halted his rig at the intersection long enough for the change of a traffic light—and long enough to change my life. Exactly what sort of change was not yet clear to me, but I knew what happened on that street corner was both splendid and irreversible.

All day, I reveled in what I suspected was the dawning of my womanhood, eager to share the marvel with my mother. When I arrived home, she was at the kitchen counter unpacking groceries, and I began to tell what had happened at the bus stop. Mom glanced over at me—and my outfit—then quickly turned back to her work. Without allowing me to finish my story, she began to lecture sternly that my legs were too long for miniskirts and I shouldn't borrow clothing from friends. She ordered me to fold and put away the empty grocery bags as she put the food away, all the while dousing me with terms like "lustful eyes" and "objective gawking." Finally, she turned to look me square in the eye and said, "And it's about time you know men are always after only one thing."

I dutifully proceeded to launder and iron the skirt before returning it to Nancy. I waited out the wash and dry cycles in the gloomy, damp basement. Perched at my father's workbench, chin in hands, I recalled how much simpler life was when he'd set me on this revolving stool and spin me round and round until I was dizzy with delight. And now, I thought, here I am, washing the wonderful out of this day and pressing the magic out of that skirt.

After supper, I met Nancy in the alley to return the skirt. We sat on the old red bricks with knees pulled to our chests, watching the sun go down. Oblivious to the bells of St. Leo's, we speculated on the possible definitions of the "one thing" that men are always after.

"I really had to have it!" Julie repeated, reeling me back into the present. She spun around again. "Soooo, really, Mom—what do you think?"

I felt the need to tread softly at this crossroads where from underneath the oversized T-shirts and baggy jeans of last year had emerged a young woman with a waist and hips and starry eyes who was . . .

"Lovely!" I said. "You can't practice your cartwheels in it, but the skirt—and you—are lovely."

The importance of unread newspapers had grown pale in my lap. I shifted layers of newsprint aside and reached out from my bed to offer Julie the kind of hug she sometimes pretended to have outgrown. I asked if she'd like to walk with me along the parkway after dinner—to where the path winds down to the river, where the lingering sunsets this time of year can be particularly bright.

"Can't, Mom," she said, as she glanced approvingly at herself in the full-length mirror. "I already made plans with Andrea."

Oh, and so, I called my mother instead.

# Is That You, Miss C?

Virginia Read
Marco Island, FL

It was warm for this early in the year. She kicked off her covers and rolled over onto her back. The sheer curtains puffed lazily in and out from the slight breeze coming in through the open window of her apartment. She enjoyed the breeze fingering her naked body, but it did little to cool it. She should get up, but it was pleasant to lie here listening to the birds chatter in the dogwood tree outside the window.

She decided to celebrate this spring morning by wearing her pretty pink-and-white-flowered dress with the frilly collar and ruffles down the front. The pink pumps and the big pink bow for her hair would be the perfect accessories. She knew flowery, frilly, billowing dresses and bows were not what a 222-pound woman should be wearing, but long ago she had decided to wear what she loved and let the rest of the world think what they wanted to think.

Sliding her legs over the side of the bed, she sat up. Without reaching for her robe, she stood and padded through the living room to the door of her apartment. Before dressing, she always retrieved the New York Times outside her door and carried it back to the kitchen to work its crossword puzzle while eating breakfast.

Opening the door partway, she bent down and reached for the paper. No paper. She stretched her arm out as far as she could and waggled it back and forth across the floor. No paper.

That paperboy! She wanted to throttle him. Time after time, she'd asked him to leave her paper right at her door and not throw it from the stairway. Opening the door wider, she poked her head out to see on which side of the door it had landed. No paper. Stepping into the hall, she saw her paper lying halfway down the hall almost to the next apartment. This was really too much. She would complain to the paper this time.

The hall was empty. It was still early. No one on her floor was up yet. Looking both ways, she stepped out and dashed down the hall. Just as she bent over to pick up the paper, she heard a door slam. Panicked, she grabbed the paper and ran back to her apartment. The door was closed.

She grabbed for the knob and twisted. Too late, she remembered she had not switched the lock on the door to unlock. She leaned against the door and tried to think. What to do? Her mind raced over her options.

The sleazy-eyed janitor had a key, but he was four flights down. No way was she going to walk nude down four flights of stairs. Besides, he was always finding excuses to get in her apartment. Even meeting him in the hall he would look popeyed down her bosom and try to rub up against her. The janitor was out.

Jeff, in the next apartment, worked a late shift and usually slept with earplugs and eyeshades until midafternoon. It was doubtful that pounding on his door and shouting would rouse him, but it would certainly rouse the rest of the floor.

The apartment across the hall belonged to the snooty Van Duzens. They found it difficult to even say good day. The last time they had met in the hall, the woman pointedly said, "You should use less rouge on your cheeks and wear more appropriate dresses. You look like a whore. People will think this is a brothel." What would she think now?

The apartment next to them belonged to Tom, a newly divorced man. Shortly after he'd moved in, he'd knocked on her door with drinks in hand. "Just want to be friendly," he said. Once inside, he became friendly all right. She definitely wasn't going to ask him for help.

The retired professor in the end apartment was her only hope. He wore a black patch over one eye. Supposedly his vision was impaired. Hopefully, his sexuality was too, but that was somewhat dubious. He left early every morning to eat breakfast and read his paper at the drugstore on the corner. She suspected that the young girls going to school and the young women on their way to work were the real attraction. Nevertheless, he was her best choice. There was nothing to do now but wait until he made an appearance.

While she waited, she tried to fashion some sort of covering from the pages of the Times. She wrapped several sections around her, trying to position them to cover her ample flesh. The pages either kept slipping down or tore. Torn, crinkled paper covered her feet, and with only two hands, it was impossible to cover her boobs and lower parts at the same time.

She decided that when she heard someone in the hall, she would turn and face the wall. That way she wouldn't have to look at anyone and they would only see her back. She hoped she wouldn't have to stand here much longer. Goosebumps covered her body but did little to hide anything. Hearing the noise of a door opening and closing, she quickly turned and faced the wall. With closed eyes, she listened as the steps came closer and then stopped.

"Is that you, Miss C?"

"Yes, it's me."

"Well, good morning to you. I'm on my way to the drugstore for my paper and breakfast. Have a nice day."

"Professor, I need you to do something for me."

"I'll be happy to do what I can to help a lady. Leave a note for me in my mailbox."

"NO! Don't go. I need you to help me right now."

"Are you in trouble, Miss C?"

"Yes. I'm locked out of my apartment."

"Well, I'm sorry to hear that, Miss C."

"I need a key to unlock my door."

"I'm sorry, Miss C, but I don't know anything about locks. If your apartment's locked, you better talk to the janitor."

"That's what I want you to do. I want you to ask the janitor for the key to my apartment."

"It's nice of you to offer to give me your key, but I think it's better if we keep our own keys."

"I don't want your key. I just want the janitor's key to my apartment."

"I don't know why you need two keys, but I'll be happy to tell the janitor you want another key."

"I don't want another key. I need you to ask the janitor for his key to my apartment and have you bring his key up to me."

"I'll be happy to do that. Always ready to help a damsel in distress. I'll stop on my way back from my morning errands and pick it up."

"Professor, I need that key right now. NOW! Not later."

"Well, things are usually better by tomorrow."

The sound of his squeaky shoes echoed in the empty hall. She turned in time to see his head disappear as he made his way down the stairs.

# Stealth Love

Lora Hyler
Glendale, WI

"I don't believe he's gon' die!" she exclaimed, her voice a raspy whisper. "We've been together nigh on forty-seven years, and it seems to me if you've been with somebody that long, you would know if they was gon' die."

She rolled her rheumy eyes toward her tall, slender niece, Lonnie, who fought back tears. The anxious look of the elderly black woman told the story her parched lips wouldn't tell. Her chocolate face was etched with wrinkles made more pronounced in recent weeks. The strain of too many nights spent alongside her beloved Arch's hospital bed had taken their toll. Ruthie sighed deeply, rolling her eyes toward the lone window in the bleak hospital room. The brightly colored floral arrangements and cards beckoning "Get well soon!" seemed mocking of the room's despair.

Ruthie sighed again, and it seemed to Lonnie the room exhaled with her. Lonnie thought how her aunt's once lively and mischievous eyes now appeared sunken. Nearly defeated. The layers of healthy fat that had once adorned her portly frame for as long as Lonnie could remember had deflated.

But despite the dropped shoulders, she embodied perseverance. Lonnie knew that spirit. African-American women had carried that indomitable spirit within for centuries. Lonnie smiled without realizing it.

"I've been coming up here twice a day." Her aunt's declaration jarred Lonnie back. "I used to come three or four times a day, but it got to be too much. I try to get here early before they start poking and prodding him where he's too tired to answer me when I call his name."

Lonnie nodded with bowed head.

"I come to clean the mucus out of his eyes and his nose, and sometimes . . ." A gleam entered the seventy-year-old eyes. "Sometimes, he recognize me and say, 'Ruthie, Ruthie, is that you?' Then I'll grab his hand and squeeze it to make sure he know it's me."

Lonnie sniffled imperceptibly. The prone figure on the bed reliant on beeping monitors was foreign to her.

The lean, proud former army soldier always appearing much taller than his five-foot-six frame was now a cruel replica of his former self.

Lonnie nearly failed to recognize the kind man with the gentle smile who had patiently taught her to drive. She felt her heart leap as she thought of him clinging onto the sides of his seat with a grim look as she negotiated curves far too fast for his old '72 Chevy Malibu. Though he must have had to bite his tongue, he said nothing for fear of hurting the feelings of his sensitive, beloved niece, his sister's middle child. His favorite.

Lonnie's aunt Ruthie and uncle Arch hadn't had any children of their own, choosing instead to lavish their attention on Lonnie and her two siblings, assorted other nieces and nephews, and neighborhood children. Many of these were what Arch used to call "daytime orphans" who roamed the streets as their parents attempted to eke out a living.

Times weren't always easy for the town's small black population. Most had migrated from the South during the 1940s, and while Racine, Wisconsin, offered more than southern towns, times were hard if you were black. Even when Ruthie and Arch were forced to ration their meat to have enough to stretch out for the week while Arch waited to be called back to the auto factory, he wouldn't hesitate when the melodic sounds of the ice cream truck beckoned.

Under Ruthie's fierce glare, he would raid the cookie jar, always grabbing an extra dollar or two to share the truck's bounty of assorted ice cream delights with the gaggle of expectant faces he knew would greet him in front of the truck. "Aw, Ruthie," he would chastise in his mild, soft manner. "Ain't no reason that chile shouldn't git a cone just 'cause his momma and daddy off to work."

With that he'd scoop up the change from the bowl by the door and head out. The children would greet the approach of the lean, kindly man with the slight gait with excited jumps and occasional whoops of joy, content in knowing the rich, cold custard would soon be theirs to enjoy. He seldom let them down. He got as much joy out of buying ice cream for the children as he did eating it himself.

When he reentered the small, picturesque cottage he and Ruthie had scrapped and saved to buy when they came to the auto town, Ruthie couldn't help but smile. Her beloved would always have a special treat for her besides a cone of her own—a well-placed kiss as he announced, "More sugar for my sweet."

Ruthie would grunt and as gruffly as she could muster even as a smile threatened to escape, would say, "Give me that cone, you old fool."

Lonnie had often witnessed that scene. The memories came flooding back. She realized with a start that her aunt hadn't moved in some time.

"Auntie Ruthie?" she called softly.

"Yeah, I'm here."

"Oh, I thought you might have fallen off to sleep."

"No, but Lord knows, chile, I'm tired." Ruthie sighed deeply as if to punctuate her words. "I don't always sleep too good. I'm used to somebody bein' next to me . . ." Her voice trailed off pitifully. "But I'm glad you come, Lonnie. God only know if he'll last through the summer."

Lonnie's dark head bobbed quickly. Her lean but shapely frame had sagged since she entered the room. Her heart-shaped, smooth, cream-colored face and large almond eyes had darkened. "I wanted to come, Auntie. I'm here for both of you," Lonnie said, her voice quivering. She swallowed hard, grabbing her aunt's hand. Ruthie managed a weak smile, giving her niece's hand a slight squeeze.

Moments passed. The small private hospital room felt to Lonnie like a prison cell. "Why? Why?" the voice inside her head called. But she knew there was no answer. Grief had come to visit, resting solidly upon their hearts like an unwelcome visitor who knew neither time nor boundaries. Grief was large, foreboding, and knew no master but death sure to be following closely behind.

"Why don't I take you home for a little rest? Uncle Arch will be all right by himself for a while." Lonnie suddenly felt the need to remove herself from the room.

Ruthie raised eyes too tired to protest. Shifting her eyes from Lonnie to Arch, she noticed as if for the first time that he was sound asleep. She nodded and moved as if to stand. Lonnie quickly moved to her assistance, happy to be mobile and excited to be leaving. A wave of guilt engulfed her. She quickly pushed it aside as she thought of how the brief minutes she just spent paled in comparison to the weeks her aunt had languished here in the dank hospital room.

As her hand contacted the soft, mushy flesh, Lonnie saw a woman who had aged during the agony of watching her husband begin the sonorous march away from her. Her aunt lurched awkwardly on her arthritic knees toward the bed. "Bye, Arch," she breathed. With effort, she raised her eyes toward Lonnie and attempted a weak smile. Raising a wrinkled, arthritic hand, she ran it along Lonnie's smooth face.

Lonnie's heart rose. For the first time since she had entered the hospital room, she felt as if everything would be all right.

# The Existential Poet

Sara Burr
Middleton, WI

Think about the tiniest abstraction.

A single letter: I.

Now add that character to another, and another.

Knead them like clay into words.

Line them up: y-axis by x-lines, invent a poem.

Open up its metaphor with sights, sounds, smells.

Place it under your reader's gaze.

Measure the feeling of a single sigh

And let that be the voice of the universe.

Let us listen to its meaning together.

Yes, let all our letters bring us

From nothingness into being.

# Between Then and Now

Sara Sarna
Oconomowoc, WI


The chattering child that was me

grasps my hand with jam-sticky fingers

coaxing me backward with the promise

of play.

I had forgotten

that I was her

that she was me

that we had parted

And I don't know the way back

to the time before I mothered my mother

feared my father

learned best behavior was a survival skill

Back to days heavy with honey-sweet sunshine

daisy chains and swing sets

and a secret apple tree perch.

The time between clings like cobwebs
and the trail back twists
until even the child is lost.
This is the price for playing it safe
for boundaries uncrossed
choices I can't change
that left me cocooned in caution
ill-equipped to leap.
The child was brave/I was brave
then I wasn't.
She waits
the courage of yesterday in her eyes.
There is no risk in retreat.
I breathe in and blow the cobwebs
scatter the clouds
take the hand of the child that was me
and step forward.

# Legacy

Joanne Nelson
Hartland, WI


If I take a cup from the cupboard,
the blue-lipped ceramic one, say,
careful of the glued-on handle—smoothed-over mistake—
does my cortex or whatever whisper directions?
Close your hand here, lift from the shelf now

Does each action have a past?
What guides me through this yellow kitchen?
Am I my mother moving through hers,
only a color scheme apart?

My unwitting daughter believes the choices are still hers.

Wipe the counter clockwise, keep the towels hidden, bacon grease in a jar, apples in a bowl, napkins at the ready.
Coffee beans and a piece of chocolate in the freezer.

Your life is not your own. Just try cleaning the counter this way instead of that. Listen as the dishes crash.

# Portrait of David Forsyth

Barbara Germiat
Appleton, WI

He was rectitude's model,
   straight and proper, stern, forbidding.
He was the stern of the ship of family
   that sailed on over the years.
He was a sail into the future,
   a future where his portrait came, finally, to live here
where a live descendant carried on
   the line of his genes.

He was one in a line of British gentlemen
   intent on their standing and status.
He was standing in the pantheon of
   well-dressed men, men of substance,
their substance proved by the oil paint
   of their portraits, rigid, thin-lipped, formal.
Their formal pose showed they had money
   and commanded their circumstances,

circumstances hard-won and comfortable
   yet never secure enough
that David could sit securely
   and prove he'd earned a right,
a right that came with no warranty
   but hovered unwarranted over his head,
head limned in rectitude. He showed not a hint
   of halo.

# Racing into Rain: A Midwestern Metaphor

Mike Orlock
Sturgeon Bay, WI

The road we've blithely cruised
is straight and bathed in sky
so blue it seems certain
heaven sent,
asphalt white as scalp
perfectly parting farm fields
flush with fertile growth
as Wisconsin pulls us
tethered into its green promise.

Ahead in hazy distance
the highway bends to the right
gently, then sharply,
into lowering purple skies dark
with grumbling thunder
slashing lightning strikes and winds!
winds of change
so vindictive the land and its people
will lay stunned and sundered,
bruised and scraped red raw
by a storm few ever saw coming

# My Grandma's Orange

Chris Roerden
Greensboro, NC

I dislike the taste of an orange. One sip of orange soda puckers my mouth, and my rare lick of orange ices, tempted by thirst, produces an impolite eewww. And occasionally persuaded to just try a freshly peeled segment of the actual fruit ends in an actual shiver.

But the slight scent of an orange, the barest whiff of its delicate perfume, sends me back sixty-plus years to the Bronx and my grandparents' apartment on Walton Avenue. Their ground-level three rooms saw little daylight. Even on the sunniest days their bedroom remained dark, its rear window facing a narrow alley that offered but one view: the metal-guarded ground-floor windows of the apartment building next door.

Whenever my parents took me along to visit, and the adults settled in the kitchen to talk in a language I never learned, I headed straight to that back bedroom.

In a corner near the sunless window stood my grandma's simple vanity table. Among her few objects on it sat an orange, perfect in color, size, and shape—even convincingly dimpled all over its hard, plastic surface. It also had a horizontal cut all around its middle.

Barely aware of the hum of Yiddish from the kitchen, I would stand at the vanity and carefully remove the top half of that orange orb, revealing three of the smallest glass jars I'd ever seen. Slipping seamlessly into the magic of imagination, I became a doll, those three little bottles mine. Surely no one but a doll could possibly make use of such tiny treasures.

I don't know how long I remained there breathing the slight scent, merely looking, disturbing nothing, uninterested in removing any of the minuscule caps to release the perfume within. Perhaps in playing my role I realized the dexterity required to unscrew a cap was beyond the capabilities of a doll's fingers. Perhaps my restraint reflected a little girl's desire to prevent a scolding. Much more likely was my understanding that I had no need to open anything, since the subtle whiff of orange had already captured me, its gentle fragrance sufficient to sustain my fantasy.

This corner of the bedroom, dimly lit, orange infused, became my special place each time I visited—so unlike the big, busy, open area behind the store of my other grandparents, the ones whose last name sounded like mine but a bit longer, my father having years earlier Americanized his.

Whenever my parents took me to the store for a visit, I knew I'd have to struggle against being hugged by my grandfather, a too-friendly big bear whose bristly white beard scratched my cheek. I also knew I could ignore the opposite reception from my bony, birdlike grandmother, who never touched me or smiled at me or spoke to me, or seemed at all aware of the existence of her youngest grandchild.

The drafty, gloomy store under the Jerome Avenue El sold mirrors and custom window shades. From the side walls hung mirrors of every size. The small ones remained flat against the wall, but the oversized ones that hung far above my head from thick cords, further burdened by the weight of gigantic frames ornately gilded, tilted themselves forward to look down at me and reflect back an image I wanted not to see.

I didn't linger in the storefront but trailed my parents through the darkness at the rear into the large open space that served as living quarters. The only objects available to keep me entertaining myself were decorative shade pulls. These ornaments lived in a massive chest of drawers parked in the center of the area like a room divider, where I would stand quietly in front of an open drawer, picking up and turning over each miniature: tassels in all colors, crocheted circles, two-dimensional painted teakettles, flat flowerpots sporting flat flowers. After handling the entire supply of shade pulls, I discovered that I'd been pretending . . . nothing. Not one of those fanciful objects ever engaged my imagination.

Maybe it was the room, too large and too open, bereft of a shadowed, quiet corner, each family member visible under bright ceiling lights, where along one wall my white-haired grandmother busily prepared a kosher meal while the other adults sat around the one table, their voices increasing in volume each time an elevated train roared overhead, causing the water glasses to shake and the two sets of dishes in the cupboards to rattle and each pot and pan and the building itself to tremble.

I wondered but never asked how the huge, gilt-framed mirrors hanging in the storefront hadn't leapt from the walls.

Maybe what managed to inspire my own magical imagination was the dim light of my favorite grandparents' bedroom, the distant hum of conversation, and the slightest scent of citrus. I handled nothing on my grandma's simple vanity other than removing, then eventually replacing, the top of her fragrant fake orange that had never grown in the sun.

# Covenant

Nancy Bauer-King
Racine, WI

Some days, through window glass rippled with age, I saw Ginny hurry down the porch steps and begin her purposeful walk. On August 8, 1966, Ginny's husband, Fred, had been shot down over North Vietnam, and she was informed he was listed as missing.

For six years, Ginny didn't know if her husband was alive or dead.

During those flinty years, Ginny, her young daughter, Julie, and her son, Eric—born six weeks after his father was captured—lived with her parents in a large Victorian home across the street from me. Ginny's father, a man whose arms opened easily for hugs, was well known and respected in the community. Though sagging with the burden of his daughter's distress, he readily shared news about the young family. Neighbors passed on the information in solemn tones.

"She walks every day," Mr. Burton said. "I suppose it helps her clear her mind."

"She talks to a counselor," Mrs. McCarragher claimed. "I can't imagine what she is going through."

I greeted Ginny when I saw her, but afraid then to raise the issue of anyone's suffering, including my own, I didn't initiate any extended conversation with her.

Then one shimmering afternoon, Ginny learned her husband was alive and being held in a prison camp in North Vietnam.

The news of Fred's survival winged swiftly through town. Friends, family, and neighbors hurried to the ecstatic household. Television news vans sped down Highway 41 from Green Bay. Reporters, hoisting cameras on their shoulders, loped up the front porch steps and rushed into the house.

With tears pooling in my eyes, I ran across the street to join the celebration and was met at the door by Ginny's father, who had a bottle of champagne in his right hand and an empty glass in his left. When he saw me, he began pouring the champagne into the glass and then promptly extended the drink to me.

I stopped short at the threshold. Stuck in a black-and-white commandment, I needed to make a decision. Quickly.

"Nancy," my father warned. "Don't ever taste alcohol. One out of every seventeen people becomes an alcoholic. The only way you can be sure you won't end up a drunk is not to take that first sip." Towering over me, he added, "Hundreds of brain cells die with each swallow."

At eight years old, I didn't question my father's statistical evidence. But I did picture myself lying disheveled in a gutter, a bottle clutched tightly to my ravaged body.

My father carried temperance literature in his dress shirt pocket and wouldn't go into restaurants that served the lethal liquid. He carefully cut out all the car-crash articles from the Janesville Gazette that included alcohol. He waved them in front of the driver's ed students and thumbtacked them to the bulletin board in his high school science classroom.

After one of his "Evils of Alcohol" talks at church, my father was accosted by my Sunday school teacher.

"Jesus drank wine," Mr. Olson argued.

"He didn't drive down the highway at fifty-five miles per hour," my father retorted. Case closed. Methodists were not supposed to drink or smoke or play cards on Sunday.

Or have any fun.

On June 15, 1955, during a consecration service at summer church camp, I signed a covenant: With the help of God, I hereby promise to refrain from the use of any and all alcoholic beverages and to encourage others so to do.

I pasted my deal with God in the front inside cover of my Bible.

I had kept my promise faithfully ever since.

Still standing at the door of decision, I looked past the champagne that Ginny's father offered me. I saw Ginny, sitting in a wingback chair and surrounded by people who had walked miles and years of a bleak unknown with her. They were sipping and laughing and hugging and wiping wet cheeks. A floor lamp near Ginny spread a golden light across her face and throughout the room.

I took the champagne and stepped out of a black-and-white covenant into a richer, more colorful life of uncertainty.

# On Their Own Terms

Nancy Jesse
Madison, WI

Sarah Foster unlocked the door, turned on the light, and inhaled the smell of her parents. Cigarette smoke. And the French lavender her mother set out in bowls to mask odors. Earlier that morning, the lawyer had given Sarah their keys and told her to take anything she wanted. But she only had an hour. After that, Golden Estate Sales would sort, assess, and set out for sale her parents' earthly possessions.

It looked so tidy. Clearly her father, always thinking ahead, had cleaned the ashtrays and cleared out the bottles, recycled newspapers, and plumped the pillows before administering the morphine. First to her mother. Then to himself.

Her father had left a note in the will. Sarah had an hour to go through their things and take what she wanted. Then all would be sold and go to named charities. Sarah understood this, understood that her father wanted to be considered by strangers as part of some perfect good because he couldn't deal with the imperfections of his life. His stalled career in Madison. His falling in love with and marrying his first cousin. Sarah, his accidental only child, who'd always disappointed him. In the end, he'd left her no part of their estate except what tokens she could take in an hour.

Sarah sized up the room: the familiar orange couch, old-fashioned even when she was growing up; teak bookshelves stuffed with art books; two winged chairs with matching sagging ottomans. Not much for her in this room. If she took any furniture, she'd have to rent a U-Haul, have to stuff it into her studio apartment. No. She'd take no heavy objects that meant little to her. Instead, she pulled out a slim volume on Jackson Pollack from a bookshelf. Her father's spidery handwriting littered the margins. Sarah's hand trembled as she set the book in her bag.

When Sarah was seven, she'd lived with her grandmother for a year while her parents were on sabbatical in Berlin. When they'd returned, her father had given her a copy of Goethe's Faust in German. He told her it was a rare old manuscript that she would grow to appreciate. She did. In her twenties, Sarah had sold it to a book collector. She'd used the money to buy a little blue Nova, the car she still drove in Madison.

Opening the hall closet, Sarah found a folding wheelchair and a yellow mohair sweater permeated with her mother's perfume, L'Air du Temps. Her father must have given the rest of the clothes away. They would never fit Sarah anyway; her mother had been tiny. She couldn't resist, though, caressing the fabric. Maybe if she lost a little weight. Slipping the sweater off the hanger, she tried it on, felt the material strain at her shoulders, the sleeves end at the elbows. Tugging it off, she carefully folded the sweater before setting it on the shelf.

The door of the bedroom she kept closed. No need to go there—where her parents had left on their own terms. She leaned her cheek against the cold doorframe, pausing for a minute or two. She'd always been so different from them, feeling like a distraction from their devotion to each other. She knew her father wanted to be kind, to save her mother from the slow drip of dementia. Save himself from the fearsome loneliness of the widower. The debasement of old age.

The last day she'd seen her parents, her father had served up bowls of Cream of Wheat laced with honey and nuts. Her mother had slept through the meager lunch. Sarah and her father took their meal standing. Afterward, she trimmed his beard, one of those little chores he entrusted to her. Then he'd told her his plans—where he kept the vials of morphine, how much he'd need for each of them, how he'd work out all the technicalities. Sarah had told him she didn't think this was legal, asked him—begged him really—not to do this to her mother, who could no longer speak for herself. He said he had discussed it with Mother when she had all her faculties. That she was completely in accord with him. Did she, Sarah, want to be with them at the end? She refused. Her father had said, "Suit yourself."

Sarah moved to the kitchen, glancing at the clock above the sink. Twenty minutes left. To save time, she opened all the cupboards and drawers and then stood back to evaluate the contents. The Limoges china with its tiny roses she detested, recalling long afternoons after her mother's luncheons, hand washing the pieces whose gold rims wouldn't hold up in the dishwasher.

The set of ivory-handled steak knives tempted her, but she'd never get them past airport security. Most meals she ate out, so no need for mixing bowls, cake pans, the Cuisinart.

Then she spotted her mother's favorite martini glass, the funky one with the stem bent into three angles for easier handling, especially after the third or fourth drink. Threads of gold and red ran through the bowl in an abstract pattern, not unlike a Pollock. A small chip marred the base—but what better way to remember her mother, recklessly spirited at cocktail time? And her father, who believed a good martini could solve all problems. One of the few things Sarah and her father agreed on.

It was while they were drinking martinis that Sarah's mother had told her about her birth. Her father has been terribly frightened by it all, her pain in labor, the bloody helpless infant, his utter lack of control. He'd spent the night after her birth at the Edgewater Bar, watching a storm over Lake Mendota. Sarah's mother had promised to never have another child. But she wanted Sarah to know, above all, that she, her only child, was the one great love of her life. Her mother had loved Sarah more than life itself. And she wanted Sarah to understand that her father had done all he could to do right by them.

Sarah wrapped the glass in paper towels and stuffed it in her bag. Five minutes left to get the key back. At the airport, she'd spend a couple hours drinking to her parents at the bar. Communion with her mother's chalice. The last tribute to her parents' fierce love. She would come to some understanding, she told herself. Not flinch. Not fall apart. But reconcile. Already she could imagine the cool gin turning to warmth, spreading through her stomach, chest, and arms.

Sarah switched off the light and locked the door. The hallway was so quiet she could hear her own footsteps. Walking away, she felt a lightness, a steadiness. This must be, she thought, the peace of the dead.

## Riding the Number 19 Bus

Nancy Rafal
Baileys Harbor, WI

I am the minority
        old white woman
this morning and every morning
        dark-skinned women   silky headgear and long sheer fabric
        boys of color   backpack-burdened
        Spanish speaking mother      two tired pre-schoolers in tow
        young adult males hopelessly going nowhere again and again

Somehow this morning
        the first hint of warming sun in four days
somehow it seems
        despite earbuds, empty bellies, cellphones
somehow it seems

We are all traveling in the same direction

## Fears? Not!

Greg Peck
Janesville, WI


She's trained them well,
their mother has.
If a creepy crawls,
they'll scamper and scoot.
Should a bee or fly
or skeeter draw near,
they'll duck and dodge
and dart for the door.
They go overboard.
"Eek! A spider!
"Help, Papa," they'll
plead to their grandpa.
"I nearly died
"from that black widow,"
their mother justifies.
An arachnophobe, as a result.

And reasonable? Sure.
But she fans childhood fears
into near paranoia.
Ah, but Papa gets the last laugh.
He took the oldest
on a boat when she
was barely past diapers.
He taught her to fetch
a worm or even—
don't look Mom—a leech.
This granddaughter did so
and still fears not today.
She even caresses the critter,
before her Papa
impales it on a fish hook
and tosses it overboard.

# The Girls with the Grandmother Faces

Marjorie Pagel
Franklin, WI

Thirty years ago, an ardent feminist,
I bristled when anyone referred
to my friends and me as "girls."

Now, though, I just smile.
There's a group of us – pals since high school –
who get together now and then.
We are, like the title of that book,
the "girls" with the grandmother faces.

You cannot tell in the Facebook photo
which of us are widows,
which losing eyesight or hearing. Or who is
bearing up in spite of illness, sorrow . . .
worries about children, grandchildren, husbands.

We are all smiling into the camera
with brave and joyful faces,
celebrating friendships
of half a century.

# The Light

Shirley Barker
Bay View, WI

The melancholy morning clenched me with clammy forearms.

I writhed and pried to succor freedom to go about my way.

Although held fast I refused to succumb to its insolent terms.

Seemingly a plane's raucous roars rend the somber veil, expelling light of day.

I halted at the unexpected gleam that breached my sight.

It craved that I ever be a prisoner of its morose pit,

But light awakened courage's bounty to fight.

Deliverance path shown open ready to trek and lit.

Every fiber within incited me to alter my desperate estate.

Riving free of gloom's steely grip I rushed to the beaming light.

I sprinted from the pit's imminent doom before it was too late.

The revelation of light birthed the vigor for my urgent plight.

My mind's internal light, yet again, rescued me from depression's pitfall

Escaping once more, I can persevere in life—absent the black wall.

# Peacemaker

Raymond Schrab
Hartford, WI

Air gets thin and cold at 50,000 feet. On Day 1 of the operation, it slid by the cockpit at 600 miles per hour. Inside the cockpit was Captain John Jones, known to family and friends as Johnny. Clad in black pressure suit and mask, he swung his head stiffly to the right. There was his copilot, Lieutenant Logan, dressed the same. He knew they looked like some kind of giant bugs invading from outer space. The drone of eight turbojet engines slung out below 185-foot wings was interrupted by a crackle of radio.

"Raider One, Raider One, what is your status. Over."

"All is go. Checklist complete. Green lights across the board. Over."

"Do you have visual on all other birds. Over."

Pilot and copilot swung around to count their companions, ten other giants flying in perfect formation. Captain Jones marveled at the sight of it. Here were eleven B-52 bombers, technology of the 1950s, but flying into harm's way in the twenty-first century.

"Affirmative. Over."

"Understood. You may proceed. Good hunting."

In moments, hundreds of dark bomblets were falling toward Earth, gravity drawing them inevitably to their target point in the troubled African nation below.

Two ancient pickup trucks with obligatory fifty-caliber machine guns mounted in their beds skidded to a stop in the sand. Five men with Kalashnikovs jumped out and rushed up to the debris. It looked like some sort of smashed plastic barrel with clumps of moss scattered around. The men spread out and began inspecting others like it randomly spread across the desert. After confused discussion, they dragged some of the debris into their trucks and headed back to base.

On Day 3, Sergeant Gomez was on the job in a hardened bunker one hundred feet beneath endless wheat fields somewhere in Kansas. He stared intently at the big screen monitor as he worked the joystick with his right hand. He clutched a tall, narrow blue-and-silver can of Red Bull in his left. Seven thousand miles away, his drone circled and spied, checking events on the ground. Seen from directly overhead, three tiny dots appeared to be chasing a larger group of dots. Upon boosting magnification, he saw it was three men with machine guns firing at hapless people running before them. There were bursts of sand jumping up around those fleeing, and two victims fell suddenly to the ground. Gomez cringed, as did the base commander standing ramrod straight behind him.

"So far results are negative, Commander."

"Yes, Sergeant, but keep a close eye on things."

The drone fed video, of course, but no audio, so for the men in Kansas everything played out in silence. They couldn't hear the machine guns firing, nor when the firing stopped. They could only take notice, after a few moments, that the little bursts of sand around the feet of the fleeing victims ceased. Gomez zoomed in on the three men with weapons, saw them shaking and inspecting their guns. Then all three turned, simultaneously, and ran. Swinging the camera to the larger group of people, Gomez saw the pursued had become the pursuers, chasing the three killers with rocks and big sticks in hand.

On Day 5, the mood in the Pentagon was optimistic but restrained. The staffer was all business as he briefed key members of the defense establishment, military and civilian. He addressed the Secretary of Defense.

"Sir, as you know, we have received intelligence from reliable sources on the ground indicating signs of success. Violence has fallen off dramatically in an area of some one hundred square miles in and downwind from the target areas of our airdrops, centered here. There have been noteworthy events here and here, as eyewitnesses report the terrorists have abandoned these two villages without a fight. Civilians of the area have taken control of both." He used a red laser pointer on the large map projection as he spoke.

"And no losses among our bombers as yet?"

"No, sir. The terrorists are not known to have surface-to-air missiles capable of reaching our B-52s. The concern, sir, is that as time passes their allies in the Middle East may bring missiles into our zone of operations."

"And those allies have such weaponry?"

"Yes, sir, trailer mounted SAMs, purchased from Russia."

"Still, we have an opportunity to change the game. We can end the endless wars. Gentlemen, do we agree that it's worth the risk?"

Just fifteen minutes later, at Barksdale Air Force Base in Louisiana, another flight of B-52s thundered into the air.

On Day 6, it hit the BBC. One of those plucky British reporters stared into the camera, with a dusty and dilapidated village in the background for proper effect. When the cameraman pointed at him, he began.

"Here in this tortured North African nation, we are seeing with our own eyes evidence of a dramatic new development in the warfare that has plagued this country for years. In significant stretches of countryside, violence has fallen to near zero. It seems most weapons no longer function. Machine guns don't fire. Grenades and mortars don't go off. Artillery pieces stand useless. The violence began to recede within days of reports of formations of large jets flying overhead. We do not believe this to be a coincidence. Sources tell us that some sort of agent, possibly chemical or biological, has been dropped into this area that prevents gunpowder and even modern explosives from firing off."

Two men were seated on a bench in Central Park. One was the CEO of Midnight Munitions, the other of Bacterial Solutions. One spoke quietly; the other was upset.

"Are you crazy, Dick? You could put me out of business."

"Yes, Rod?"

"I'm in the defense business, Dick. I've got my own sources. You've developed some kind of a superbug that eats explosives! It could spread all over the world! Who's going to buy my munitions if they won't blow anything up?"

"It can't spread on its own, Rod. It's genetically engineered so it can't reproduce. The only such bugs out there will be what I make. And sell, of course."

"But I'll go bankrupt. Rumors alone have brought my stock down twenty percent in two days."

"That's why we're here. I'd like to invest in Midnight Munitions."

And Dick was happy to explain. He'd teach Midnight how to develop munitions resistant to his new bugs. Then he'd mutate his bugs to eat those munitions. Then they'd develop yet newer munitions and newer bugs. They'd have a monopoly on both lines of business. It would be perfect. It would be an endless supply of profits.

On Day 14, a newly deployed SAM reached upward to where Captain Jones and his crew were flying another mission. As he released his bomblets, he knew they were making history. Even as the missile warning flashed in his cockpit, he was content. Unable to evade, he and his crew ejected. The missile blew into the giant aircraft, and the orange explosion was seen for miles. B-52 bombers have six-man crews, six ejection seats. Shrapnel found one. Captain Jones was killed instantly.

Pieces of aluminum fluttered to the ground. On one, painted in blue letters, was the name Johnny had given the old B-52.

Peacemaker.

# Hiraeth

Dan Kussart
Sheboygan, WI

The sailor looked east, to the horizon. Toward home. Cardiff, and his beloved Mary.

"Belay that wool-gathering," came a gruff voice behind, and he turned to see the captain, stern yet with a hint of twinkle in his voice. Captain knew all about coming home to loved ones, though he'd lost his own wife some twenty-odd years ago. His limbs might creak worse than the rigging above, but he remembered what it was like to be young and in love.

"The glass is dropping," the captain went on. "Looks like we're comin' home to a storm. Let's secure the ship."

They'd been through dozens of storms, this crew. Every man could do his duty without a thought. So as the sailor fastened ropes and knotted them tight, his thoughts strayed once more to home, and Mary.

A sweet little girl from Ludlow made him the envy of all the young men in Cardiff. "Watch 'er," an old shipmate had told him. "Or better still, watch yer friends. Yer gone for months; makes another fellow think he can have his way."

"Don't you worry 'bout my Mary," he'd countered. "She's truer than a trade wind."

The shipmate had looked at him as if he were either the luckiest man on Earth, or the most naïve.

A slap of rain in his face, like a bee sting, awakened him. Shipmates were shouting over the ever-increasing wind. When had the sky gone so black?

The sailor and two others were sent aloft to shorten sail against the storm. As he climbed the swaying mast, his sure hands grabbed each handhold so firm his knuckles went white. Aloft, the ship's movement was exaggerated, like a bobbing toy boat in a tub. How dreadfully sick he'd been the first few times doing this! Terror had sent acidic phlegm to his mouth. He'd bitten his tongue hard, and blood mixed with bile, and he'd gone sick over the side. Now, the mast's gyrations were familiar; he anticipated every movement.

He straddled the crossbeam, pulled on the sail ropes. The sheets were already soaked through, making them like lead weights. His heart pounded in his ears, but his powerful arms and shoulders, and vice-like hands, never weakened.

The task was done, and they clambered down. The others went below to dry off and wait out the storm. He held back.

The ever-approaching shore enthralled him. They were so close, faint dots of yellow and white light could be seen against the lowering sky. Like fireflies on a summer night.

Gave him a sense of what his Welsh parents called hiraeth: a longing nostalgia for home, and for all that entailed.

A longing for Mary.

As he stood transfixed, the wind rocked him so hard he instinctively grabbed hold of the rail. They were getting closer to shore with each passing moment. He couldn't see that; years at sea allowed him to sense it.

"A man could get hisself drownt out here," was shouted in his ear. The captain stood by his side, placed a steadying hand on his shoulder. "Best get below, lad."

The sailor grinned, rain streaming down his face. "Don't worry 'bout me, Cap'n. Got seawater in my blood."

His captain was about to reply when a great wave broke over the bow and swept him off his feet. As the wave receded and water flowed out the scuppers, the sailor rushed to help his fallen commander. The captain flailed about on the deck, fear on his face. Their ship listed badly to starboard, and the sailor slipped and fell, knocking the old man sideways, like skittles.

Black water seemed to rise up from the side to meet them, swirling like a maelstrom, drawing them down. A rope appeared from nowhere, blown loose from its bracket. It whipped right into his hand, as if placed there by God, and he automatically grabbed hold and hung on with a death grip. At the same time, he grabbed the captain's sleeve and pulled him up.

The ship stabilized, and they struggled upright, feet slipping on the swirling deck.

There was no time for thankful prayers or expressions of relief. The coast was suddenly much nearer, and the captain turned to his miserable wheelman hunkered down against the storm.

"Hard a-port!" cried the captain, but wind flung the order back down his throat.

Cursing, the captain scrambled toward the wheel, waving his arms and calling. The wheelman could barely see, let alone hear, and continued his course. His captain staggered toward the steps that led up to the wheel.

He never made it. Another wave, stronger than the first, crashed over the side, swept the captain off his feet again . . . and out to sea.

"Man overboard!" cried the sailor, but the storm just howled in derision.

The wheelman had witnessed his captain's fate, and stood in shock, let loose of the wheel, which spun madly out of control. The sailor guided himself along the rails, staggered up the stairs like a drunken man, and finally reached his stunned shipmate.

"Hard a-port!" the sailor shouted and grabbed the wheel. The other man snapped back to life and helped.

Slowly, with a groan from its bowels, the ship responded. Their course would take them, for a time, broadside to the storm, but the idea was to turn completely about and sail into it. They would make no progress, but at least their rapid approach to the shore would be slowed, if not stopped. The two veteran seamen knew this was the goal without sharing a word.

No thought was needed, just pure strength and willpower, and the sailor found his thoughts going back to Mary, to home, to hiraeth. His heart seemed to swell; he thought it might burst from his chest, and tears mingled with rain and sea. To see her once more: that was the only reason for survival now. To sit by the fire on such a night as this to listen to winds howl and rain beat down, and all the while to be home with her.

Their early progress was checked. The ship no longer responded to their desperate attempts to turn about. Sea and wind were too much. Slowly, agonizingly, the ship fought back against their efforts, until suddenly there was a loud crack below deck, and the wheel spun so wild and free, it was clear they were rudderless.

Both men tumbled to the deck when the wheel let loose, and now all they could do was cling to whatever handhold they could, and pray.

And still they neared the coast.

A grinding shriek, a jolt that shot loose their grip, and the ship lurched up, then crashed down. The world was a sea of noise, of shouting men below, of howling storm and pouring rain, of pounding surf.

And then, it suddenly ended.

The sailor lay on his back, solid ground beneath him, and though the storm raged, he could no longer hear it. A bright poke of sun, as happened sometimes in the midst of a storm, bathed his face in warmth, and there was Mary. His Mary, smiling down on him, reaching a hand to touch his battered face. He tried to lift his hand but could not. She smiled reassuringly. Then he closed his eyes and, with a smile, drifted off with hiraeth—dreams of home.

# Wash. Dry. Fold. Repeat—Sailor Style

Julia McCurdy Gimbel
Milwaukee, WI

Everyday life goes on, even when you're fighting a war. You still get up each morning and put on your pants, one leg at a time. You also have to find a way to wash those pants, and for the sailors of World War II, that is a story worth telling.

Imagine the difficulty of keeping a uniform up to snuff under the challenging conditions of war. The sheer numbers are mind-boggling; over four million Americans serving in the Navy must have created a colossal mountain of wash.

For the newly recruited seamen, the trail of laundry began in boot camp, where each man was issued all the pieces of his uniform from boxer shorts to overcoat. Each sailor received a stencil with his last name and first initial or, in some cases, last name and service number. He went to work filling in the letters with India ink to mark every single piece of clothing—even his socks. When finished, he hung the clothes on a wash line or laid them carefully on the grass to dry.

The sailors-in-training learned to pack everything they owned in one canvas seabag, following a strict procedure for doing so. Each clothing item was rolled up so tightly it looked like a small salami—maybe one and a half inches around. Foot-long cords with crimped metal tips were tied on either end of the cylinder to secure it. One bonus of correctly rolling your clothing was that in the process you were pressing it too. A well-packed seabag could stow a fellow's whole wardrobe if it was loaded properly, so the men endured countless drills until they had the process down pat.

For most new seamen, their ship assignment came by the luck of the draw—the type of vessel you ended up on determined how you would later take care of your dirty clothes.

The larger ships in the United States fleet had their own laundry facilities right on board. For that matter, many also had their own stores, post offices, tailor shops, barbershops, and even cigar lockers. If you made your home on such a vessel, you placed your carefully labeled clothing in a bag and sent it to the laundry for washing. As easy as that.

However, the men like my dad serving on the smallest ships in the Navy, the landing craft, tank (LCTs), had none of these luxuries and had to make do on their own. Demonstrating a hefty dose of ingenuity, the crews on these flat-bottomed landing crafts successfully completed all their chores, including the laundry.

Slow-going LCTs were designed to operate along the shoreline with a range of only about five hundred miles. Even so, some began their journey by following orders to travel all the way from Pearl Harbor to the South Pacific on their own power as part of a larger fleet of ships.

On one such long voyage, an LCT crew improvised laundry duty by tying their clothes together with a rope and hurling it over the side. As the ship's propeller moved and churned the water, the ocean did all the work. The men later hauled up the line and laid the clothes out to dry on deck. To some degree it was clean, although the salt-encrusted fabric must have felt most unpleasant against their skin.

More often, LCTs were sent overseas in three separate parts aboard faster, larger ships and then assembled when they reached their final destination. One skipper caught a glimpse of his LCT briefly in New York before it was taken apart, the pieces of the craft divided between two different vessels for transport. While he was waiting to disembark, someone recommended he buy a washing machine in order to make his life easier overseas. He and part of his crew sailed with the bow of his LCT, the rest of his men following a few days later, the appliance carefully stored. His electrician kept that well-used machine in good repair throughout his ship's whole tour of duty.

Of course, most crews weren't lucky enough to have their own washing machine. Ordinarily, they would gather on the deck and begin by filling a large basin with water arduously pumped from the storage tanks; there was no running water on board. Then, using cakes of soap and washboards, the men would do their best to give the clothes a thorough washing before hanging them on a line to dry. Uniforms were worn infrequently, the men preferring their work clothes instead. In the South Pacific, they often went shirtless to get some relief from the blistering heat.

Operating near the shoreline gave the sailors an advantage: access to the native islanders, who in many cases were willing to do the men's laundry for them. Dad recalled years later, "We from time to time hired Filipino women to clean and press our clothes.

Everything came back in beautiful shape. The Navy suggested this was a very bad practice since the water used by the women could be infested with parasites called flukes. They might enter your body through the pores and generally head for your liver, on which they might dine for years. Liver flukes went to the liver, and heart flukes went to the heart, according to the Navy. It also was supposed to take years to develop—at age eighty-six I guess I'm safe, at least from the flukes. We reluctantly fired our laundresses."

Al Exner, a navy medic, also hired a Filipino woman to take care of his sailor whites. He recalled that they came back just perfect—the "whites as white as snow." He would meet this tiny woman at her gate where she took his soiled clothing and the soap he provided. Al thinks she probably did the laundry in the river, which helps confirm why the Navy brass frowned on the natives' washing practices.

A typical sailor's uniform included a one-square-yard piece of black silk to be tied as a scarf around his neck. Al's had a small hole in the knot from being tied the exact same way every single day. He knew it would need replacing soon, so he decided to give it to his Filipino washwoman. She was absolutely delighted to receive it, along with the soap that she kept, and later made herself a skirt out of the fabric.

Across the ocean in the Mediterranean, another LCT officer dropped off his laundry with an old Sicilian lady who clapped her hands and smiled whenever he came through her door. Like Al, William Baker contributed the soap. He and his laundress would count each piece of clothing as it came and went and agreed to the usual form of payment: two packs of cigarettes. William's washwoman always said hello as he was leaving, so he would quizzically answer hello and walk out. It wasn't until later that Baker learned that "ciao" means both hello and goodbye in Italian. She had cheerfully assumed that the word hello worked the same way in English.

Laundry is such a necessary yet mundane part of life. Most of us complain about doing it, even with today's high-tech machines. It's certainly not something that comes to mind when you think about World War II. But the experiences of these men show that fighting a war involves one day following the next, danger squaring off with monotony.

And chores!

# Big D, Little D

Mel Miskimen
Milwaukee, WI

My just-turned twenty-one-year-old son leaned over to me while passing the elitist version of Thanksgiving stuffing, the one made from scratch with real corn bread and real cranberries. The other version was something we called White Trash Stuffing. It's main ingredients? Gooey, cheap white bread and mayo. It was the one everyone pretended not to like but wouldn't admit that it was the one they preferred.

"Mom?" He addressed me out of the side of his mouth, like he didn't want anyone else to hear whatever it was he was about to divulge, which made me feel like all the alleged mothering wrongs I had done up to that point—the uber-nerdy sports glasses I made him wear for soccer when he was eight, the purple ladies gloves I made him wear to unload a truck because I didn't want his knuckles to get scraped—were righted because he chose me to confide in. And didn't that say something about our relationship?

I lowered my head and tucked my hair behind my ear for optimum auditory pick up.

"Mom? I'm . . . uh . . . seeing someone."

I hoped he had found a kindred spirit. Someone arty, but not incomprehensible. Someone approachable who would appreciate his romantic overtures, who wouldn't take advantage of him. Oh, who was I kidding? I wanted him to find a contemporary version of myself from thirty-five years ago. And she better not be the kind of person who would scar him for life because that was my job.

Was this the reason he hadn't friended me on his Facebook page? What was he up to? Obviously something he didn't want his mother to know about. Not friended. By my own son. Ouch!

"Is it serious?" I said.

"She seems to think so. She's . . . a doctor and—"

"A doctor?!" I said. "How long have you and she been dating?"

"What? No. No. Not seeing as in dating. No. I'm seeing her. Like, she's a shrink!" he said.

I wondered if this had something to do with when he was four and I stormed out of the house. I don't even remember what had made me lose my temper. Was this about abandonment issues?

"I'm, uh, I'm kinda depressed," he said.

Kind of depressed? Oh. Great. Another thing he had inherited from me along with droll wit, cowlicks, and bad eyes.

I had always been a worried little kid. My anxieties made worse by the perfect storm of the Sisters of Saint Joseph, Third Order of Saint Francis, and their penchant for doom and gloom and guilt and sin combined with the political world of my formative years, i.e., the Cuban Missile Crisis. And then, later on, after kids, came postpartum depression and a mental landscape of a bleak Russian winter. But that was before Prozac. And now, here was my baby boy, telling me that he, too, had the same feelings of being sucked down into a black void.

Of course it was my fault.

While the other Thanksgiving guests chitchatted over coffee and pumpkin pie, my son and I bonded over symptoms. "So, you just feel like nothing. Numb?" I said.

"Yes!" he said.

"And the world looks like an Edward Gorey illustration?"

"Oh. My. God! Yes!" he said.

He had a prescription for Paxil that he started taking while he was home, which was perfect because I could monitor him for any adverse side effects . . . "you may have thoughts about suicide when you first start taking an antidepressant such as Paxil, especially if you are younger than twenty-four years old"...

For the next couple of days, my behavior was something reminiscent of the first night after he was born, when my husband and I hovered over the crib to check if he was breathing, but ramped up a notch. Or two. Or ten.

When he sighed and got up off the sofa after pausing his zombie movie du jour and headed to the bathroom to pee, I was right there, outside the door, listening for anything that might indicate he was rummaging around the medicine cabinet for something to overdose on or cut himself with. And then when I heard the toilet flush, I had to scuttle quickly down the hallway and pretend I was dusting.

I hadn't thought twice about his choice of movie genre—the gore, the flesh-eatingness of it—but after Paxil, I thought that maybe he was getting ideas. Same thing with his musical tastes. Six months ago, I could have cared less about The Misfits or Bad Brains. Was he making an attempt at a subliminal cry for help? How would I keep tabs on him when he was ninety miles away at school? Facebook? Uh, no.

I had to drive him to the bus station, and I took advantage of my captive audience to dispense motherly (albeit co-depressive) advice: "Don't forget to take your pill. And if you forget, don't double up on the dose. I did that once. Dad and I went grocery shopping, and I kept thinking that I was dreaming that I was grocery shopping."

He nodded.

"Keep going to talk therapy because it all works together. Remember, she's there to help you."

"Uh-huh," he said.

"E-mail me. Call. Text. I can be there in an hour and a half. An hour, if I speed!"

"Mom. Don't worry. I'll be fine!"

With a wave of a hand, a roll of his eyeballs, he grabbed his man purse and bounded out of the car. Don't worry? Worrying is my hobby. That's like telling Meryl Streep not to give an Oscar-worthy performance!

Four weeks later, when he came home for winter break, he was brighter. Engaging. Like his meter had been turned two clicks to the right, out of the red danger zone and into the safe green. He talked about his classes. Exams. The papers he had to write. The professors he liked. The TAs he didn't. He wanted to study abroad. He was going to declare his major—history. He was all sunny and had cartoon bluebirds around him wherever he went.

Christmas morning we were all gathered around the tree in our matching pajama pants and mukluks (traditional gifts from Grandma). His sister, home from San

Francisco, kidded him about his sparse facial hair, my husband replenished our hot ciders, and the dog got in the way. There were paper and tape and cookie crumbs all over the place. It was one of those moments I wished I could have bottled and saved forever.

I got a lot of nice things for Christmas that year. But I have to say the best gift had everything to do with my son. It wasn't wrapped. It wasn't in a box. Or envelope. I didn't get it until three days later, when I opened my e-mails and clicked on the embedded link.

I had a friend request.

From my son.

I clicked "confirm."

## At Last

John Leighton
Hayward, WI


nothing on the desert is easy
everything has some sharp shrift
everything seems dead or dying
yet nothing dies, nothing is reclaimed
for as long as we live
the live oak will go on
remission before a slender rain
as on a surf-tormented shore
grains of golden sands creep
without the privacy of a river
or the majesty of the sea
sure, there are flamboyant times
but there is never enough

of the right kind of rain
or too much for the arroyo
life depends every day
on what can be outlasted
breath of a basilisk
outlasted is only lost
if not remembered
the loveliest remembered
is always the least looked for
and most anything planted
in this parched earth
will eventually sprout, bud, and leaf
as our ocotilla fence-work
I would burst into cloying flower
even after the wrong rain

# Trading Up

Liz Rhodebeck
Menomonee Falls, WI

The sleek, curved-edge desk
fits well in the corner,
the drawers handy, top expansive
with nooks for paper and datebook.
I bought it new, assembled out of a box –
not like the battered one rescued
from the curb one snowy night, narrow
with dark finish, curved Spanish legs,
a top that sagged in the middle;
but it was mine, a desk of my own,
secrets crammed in its sticky
drawers with ornate brass pulls,

a refuge for poems, stories and letters,
but no room for keyboards and monitors
that tilted crookedly on its surface.
Better this pull-out tray and
tower cubby, with multi-level shelves,
though I must cover the easily scratched
mock-wood finish with a pad
and the smell of glue
still lingers in the drawers –
yet, it's mine, my own desk.

But sometimes when the winter moonlight
spills across the clear uncluttered desktop,
I can hear the faint click of castanets
echo in the stillness.

## Vapor Trail

Diana Randolph
Drummond, WI

Often I fly in circles,

then propel through my home,

launching upstairs

with the laundry basket,

shoving shirts in dresser drawers,

flinging clothes in the closet.

Rushing around

doing all those tiresome tasks

as I yearn to accomplish great works—

to write novels, to paint masterpieces.

All those muted, delayed dreams
yearn to be heard.
They murmur, whisper,
then raise their voices,
releasing a roar,
trying to catch up
to align with this vehicle,
though trailing behind too slow.

Just like the swift jet
streaming across the bright-blue spring heavens
with its sound following far behind,
trying to catch up,
but appearing to hang on,
to the fading vapor trail.

## Lost in her Square

Bev Larsen
Hudson, WI

Mom feels lost in her small square.

Where is my stuff? she cries.

Her sheet music, her hymnbooks are gone.

Her crochet hooks, thread, baby yarn all missing.

She knows they are in Dad's dresser drawer,

She cannot find his dresser.

Moving day arrives; she is not ready to move.

With both feet firmly set, she hollers,

Get out of here!

I want to be alone with my stuff. Go 'way.

The door closes. She needs time. She has questions.

Where is my stool? I want my beautiful quilts.

Why must I live in this lonely square

without my iron, my vacuum, my hymnbook?

We hear her weary voice repeat,

This isn't my stuff. This isn't my stuff.

I want my yarn. Could it be in Dad's drawer?

Mom softens as the door opens.

With outstretched hands she pleads,

Where is church; where is my home?

She will not sob, she will not weep

in a house she does not know.

## She's Gone (1974)

Dan Meyer
Appleton, WI

When I heard your voice, that new song in an old building,
I thought the ocean would part ways and reveal
sunken mysteries, forgotten centuries before their answers evolved.

Songs of the mundane, tracing scattered clouds,
acting backdrop for the black plastic and sun-cracked sound
our new-car radio.
Stopping only for gas stations, restaurants, and campsites,
our minds preoccupied with old ideas
telling us what devotion looks like.

.

We tried to watch backyard trees grow like children,
blue auto paint turn to colors of rust,
backs of our hands wrinkle like the mountains we knew.

It's too easy to hate ourselves for loving
those old songs we found irresistible.

## The Poet

Evan Sasman
Ashland, WI

Sometimes I just have to throw myself into life,

roll around in it,

get dirty from it,

then carry the scent of it to others.

# The Road to Nowhere

Jane Yunker
St. Croix Falls, WI

We'd see the dust coming from miles away, towering black clouds on the horizon rolling toward us like night, moving faster than a freight train, faster than we could run, if there was anywhere to run to, which there wasn't. We'd stuff blankets under the door and hang wet sheets over the windows trying to hold it back, but still the dust came through, and soon everything was as dark inside as out. We closed our eyes and covered our mouth and nose, but still our eyes were scratched red from blinking and we coughed up black crud from deep in our chest. The tears of the children left furrows down their cheeks, like the deep gullies that now scarred our once fertile fields.

In the beginning there was anger. Men hollered and pounded their fists on the locked doors of the bank, demanding their money. If they did manage to get their hands on the bank owner, they pounded their fists into him until the law stepped in and pulled them off. But most of the time, the banker and his family were long gone before the sun rose, taking with them what little cash was in the vault, leaving the townspeople and farmers without a nickel for a loaf of bread.

Some people packed up and left, headed to the big cities of the east or west to California where it was said the sun always shines and there were jobs aplenty for those willing to work hard. First to leave were the young single men who didn't already own land of their own. Young married couples not afraid of change were quick to follow. Those who stayed behind had too much tied into what little was left of their land to just leave it all. As the years went by and still no rain fell, you could watch them die inside, one little piece at a time. You could see it in their eyes as they became dried out husks, and we children worried that one day the wind would cause them to crumble to the ground, where their ashes would mix with the blowing dust and be gone.

My older brothers left in the first wave. I would have gone with, but they said I was needed at home. They said they'd send for us as soon as they found work and a place to live. That was two years back, so I knew things must certainly be bad all over or we'd had heard by then. Mom cried every night, convinced they had come to no good at the hands of thieves and murderers. My father cursed them for abandoning us and accused them of living a sinful life of excess in the city while we slowly starved to death.

When yet another year passed without more than a spit of rain, my father announced that we were leaving Oklahoma. He'd been in town begging for a little more store credit when a stranger came in looking to buy some tobacco. The man was traveling from Arkansas to California on the promise of work for anyone willing to pick produce from sunup to sundown. My father had lost his pride long before and decided he'd much rather work as a field hand for an honest dollar than live off the charity of another man who could little afford to give it.

That next Saturday, we auctioned off the farm and whatever household goods wouldn't fit into the back of our truck for enough gas money to get us to California. Mom wrote a letter to my brothers explaining where we'd be and, not knowing where to send it, left it with our minister's wife in case they ever came back looking for us. By Monday, we were on the road to California and a new life. I sat in the truck bed looking back at what no longer was, what would never be again, clouds of dirt blowing back from the tires, and knew that what lay ahead could only be an improvement, no matter how bad it turned out to be.

# Anything

Eric Montag
Wisconsin Rapids, WI

John's wife and kids were home, so John and Duck talked in the shed. It was late and they got down to business. "The motherboard on your bot is shot," Duck informed John. "I can't fix it."

John's bronzed face was a mask, but Duck knew the weight of his own words. He also knew John's sort: no stock in the market, no education, and less money in the bank than he needed. It was John's robot that kept the family afloat, and with that robot gone, the family would sink.

John's bot, an old KAX 2500 that he had inherited from his father, specialized in mining coal. Since yesterday morning, though, it had specialized in sitting in John's garage, unmoving and humming uselessly. This of course was why John had sent for Duck. Duck could fix bots, especially the mining and lumber-cutting variety. Most of the time, he could do it quickly too, and that was what John really needed. According to contract, if John's 2500 sat idle for more than three days, Allred Mining could cancel his contract and give the work to someone else's Bot.

"And a new motherboard . . ." John said, his thought trailing off.

"Expensive," Duck replied.

John ran a hand through his dusty blond hair and looked away. "Allred won't wait. They'll jump to get out of the contract. That 2500 is sixty-two years old. There are lots of guys with newer bots. Bigger bots. I'll never get another contract."

Duck nodded.

"I could find work myself—more work, I mean. No reason a young man like me can't work more." John sounded as though he were trying to convince himself. Likely as not, John was already putting in the standard fifty-hour workweek. But his human wages were no doubt a pittance compared to what the robot brought in.

"Maybe you want to sleep on it," Duck suggested. "Talk it over with Lindy."

John turned back to him. "Three days. This is the end of day two right here."

"Got here as soon as I could," Duck replied. He did feel bad. There was very little time.

"I know," John said, and when he rubbed his chin, Duck saw his hand tremble. Duck could not imagine being in John's place, and watching it all unfold made him very glad of his dividend checks. Duck's father had had plenty of stocks, and now those stocks provided. So much so, in fact, that fixing bots had become more of a hobby than a job.

But John should have known that this day would come. Hadn't he planned for it? When Duck showed up early this morning to start working, he had seen that Lindy was obviously pregnant with their third child. How could John have gone and done that with a sixty-two-year-old KAX? John and Lindy were living far beyond their means. No man could afford three children!

"Know of anyone looking for help?" John asked.

"I know men who are looking for certain things, but nothing a good man like you will want to provide. These men would be . . . hard on your family."

John understood immediately. He looked at Duck and rubbed his face again. His eyes were wide and glassy. "They're my family," he said, choking up. "I love them. I'll do anything."

For a moment, Duck wanted to scream at the top of his lungs, "Didn't you plan for this? Have you seen what happens to the families who have no bot?" But he didn't. Instead, he said, "I know you do."

John wiped his face with his sleeve. "There's the Exchange."

Duck nodded and was glad that he had not had to be the one to say it. "That's an option."

"What do you think they would want for the new motherboard?" His eyes were wide and terrified, but he was listening. His hand brushed his chin almost constantly. "A lung? A kidney?"

Duck did not work for the Exchange, and he did not know the value that they placed on a human kidney or lung. But he knew that the motherboard that John needed easily cost more than three hundred grand. And then there was paying for installation and Duck's diagnostic work. Duck felt for John, but he was not in the business of charity. "I think you're looking at a terminal cost here."

"Jesus," John gasped.

Duck resisted the urge to put out his hand. There was no use in crying and carrying on. John was a grown man who had made his choices. And he was certainly not the first man to consider going to the Exchange. "Don't quote me, but all totaled, I should think a young, healthy man like you would be worth at least a million. I would take that money and buy a new robot. A KAX 7500 should run you about six hundred grand, and that includes the hundred-year warranty. Your son will have a nice bot that should carry him and his own child all his life. Long enough for him to save for a new bot. You'll even have money left over for Lindy to support your daughter and that baby she's carrying." Duck didn't think that she would need it, though. Lindy was still good-looking. If she was smart, she would invest the leftovers for the other two children. Get them some stock too. And then get herself a new husband.

John was still rubbing his jaw. How strange it must be to touch your own face and realize that it wouldn't be yours much longer, Duck thought. "It is the only way," John whispered.

"I'll come back in the morning. We can go together, and I can help make sure everything's in order."

John nodded, and Duck left. He heard John begin to wail even before he was halfway across the yard. Up on the porch, Lindy jumped up from her chair and came running past Duck toward the shed. She was already bawling herself.

Duck did show up the next morning, but he didn't stay long. There was a semi unloading a large crate in John's driveway. Parked next to the semi was a huge flatbed truck from Allred. Once the new bot was taken to the mine, it would continue the work of supporting John's family with good bot wages.

John still owed for diagnostic work, but Duck decided that he'd send that bill to Lindy later on. Perhaps he would even offer to take the KAX 2500 to satisfy that debt. It wasn't worth much, but he could use it for parts, and it would help John's family out. After all, Duck was a businessman, but he was not heartless.

# Critique Chic

Joel Habush
Milwaukee, WI

In the Writing Community, you will find writers in organized settings helping other writers with advice, support, constructive critique, and collegiality; if you're lucky, there might even be cookies. Most of your fellow participants try to couch their criticism in gentle ways, although running the risk of obfuscating helpful criticism.

WHEN YOU THINK THIS . . . "Every week it's the same old, same old."
SAY THIS . . . "You have a very consistent voice."

WHEN YOU THINK THIS . . . "Go buy a grammar book. And did you know there's a thing called spell-check?"
SAY THIS . . . "I just made a few line edits."

WHEN YOU THINK THIS . . . "Was that supposed to be funny? Come on. Really?"
SAY THIS . . . "Your humor is uniquely you."

WHEN YOU THINK THIS . . . "Who's talking? Who's in charge? This is a real mishmash."
SAY THIS . . . "I'm a little confused about the point of view."

WHEN YOU THINK THIS . . . "What are you, a hundred?"
SAY THIS . . . "Some of your distinctive phrases might not be picked up readily by today's readers."

WHEN YOU THINK THIS . . . "You don't remember my name, you forget where you parked your car, yet you can take a whole page to describe your mima's apron?"
SAY THIS . . . "Your detailed word pictures are so vivid that you could actually afford to cut back on some of them."

WHEN YOU THINK THIS . . . "It's a poem. A poem? What am I supposed to do with this? Should I bluff and say something about meter?"

SAY THIS . . . "I'm afraid I don't read as much poetry as I should, so I don't think I can do it justice as I try to plumb the depths of its content."

WHEN YOU THINK THIS . . . "Kill me now. I thought it was just Amazon that was involved in droning."
SAY THIS . . . "It could stand a bit of tightening."

WHEN YOU THINK THIS . . . "Your hero is a total jerk. I hope he dies."
SAY THIS . . . "Well, you've succeeded in making your protagonist strong and multifaceted. Perhaps you could help the reader by bringing to light some of his more positive attributes."

WHEN YOU THINK THIS . . . "Your dialogue sucks! Haven't you ever heard how people talk?"
SAY THIS . . . "I love your descriptions. I'd like to see more of them, even if meant sacrificing some of the dialogue."

WHEN YOU THINK THIS . . . "Enough with the interminable descriptions. Is there a story lurking in here somewhere?"

SAY THIS... "I love your dialogue. Let that carry along the piece even more, along with shifting the burden to the backstory, although it requires sacrificing much of your description."

WHEN YOU THINK THIS... "Buy a period!"
SAY THIS... "There's something almost Faulknerian in your style."

WHEN YOU THINK THIS... "Boy oh boy. I better take Thumper's father's advice here—'If you can't say something nice, don't say nothin' at all.'"
SAY THIS... "Wow. There's quite a bit here. I'd really have to mull this over before I could comment adequately. By the way, I love your outfit."

WHEN YOU THINK THIS... "I'll throw a bone in here for everybody to worry to pieces, and when they're through following my deft sidetracking, it will be time to move on and I will have dodged another bullet."
SAY THIS... "I love your use of metaphor. Or is it simile? Wait—can it be both?"

WHEN YOU THINK THIS... "What the heck are you talking about?"

SAY THIS . . . "I love, love your use of ambiguity."

WHEN YOU THINK THIS . . . "Who the heck are you talking about?"
SAY THIS . . . "I love, love your use of allusion."

WHN YOU THINK THIS . . . "Boy, this baby needs a total rewrite."
SAY THIS . . . "You might want to put this away for a while."

WHEN YOU THINK THIS . . . "Uh-oh, she's going to call on me. I've got nothing. Think, think!"
SAY THIS . . . "Why not try putting everything in the past tense?"
OR . . . "You're using the past tense; perhaps changing everything to the present tense will give the reader more of a sense of immediacy. I know it's a major rewrite for you, but we're all here to grow."
NOTE: This dodge also works with suggesting changing everything to first person, or second person, or omniscient third person.

WHEN YOU THINK THIS . . . "If you bring that piece back in here one more time, I swear I will kill myself!"

SAY THIS . . . "I think it's ready for you to submit."

WHEN YOU THINK THIS . . . "Well, whatever criticisms I've made, I can always smooth things over with a disarming smile and . . ."

SAY THIS . . . "But that's just me."

NOTE: If you're marking up a copy of the piece, this is where you put the smiley face.

## A friend speaks of her dying father

Lisa Rivero
Milwaukee, WI

In calm iambic tones she talks of failing
appetite, his taking an hour to finish
a sandwich quarter, apple slice, prevailing
by habit more than will, senses diminished,
as if he were weeding the garden for her mother at last,
fixing the forever drip in the bathroom drain
or putting up storm windows once summer has passed,
fulfilling his final duties, all that remain.
She soon will follow to a place both stark
and silent, to become herself both stark and silent,
a crocus bulb or hyacinth kept dark
by quilt of snow and earth indifferent to violence
until the unseen change of seasons tears
her open, thrusts her into grieving air.

# The Defibrillator Meal

Ed Sarna
Oconomowoc, WI

As youngsters growing up in the fifties, our Easter breakfasts were always celebrated at Grandpa's house, following the unspoken "Eldest In The Family Gets To Stay Home" rule. As the front door burst open to the scent of cigars and Polish sausage, we were quickly "Happy Easter'd" inside by Aunt Lottie so as not to let the near-atomic heat escape. Electricity was in the air—literally; most likely a combination of forced air with plastic runners and furniture covers yellow from decades of smoke.

Our family, counting Mom and Dad, totaled nine, while my uncle Bill, slacker that he was, could only muster seven. When you added in my aunt and grandfather, you came up with the optimum number of bodies for a Chicago bungalow. Unless you needed to breathe. Once inside, the men gathered around the dining room table, while the women found refuge in the kitchen, wondering aloud, as they did every year, if there was going to be enough food.

Let me digress for a moment to describe the feast, which in later years we have come to affectionately call The Defibrillator Meal. It's important to remember that this was breakfast, the first, but definitely not last, meal of the day. The centerpiece was always a boulder-sized ham surrounded by mountains of fresh and smoked Polish sausages. Dozens of garishly colored eggs, the pride of the younger kids, occupied a nicely filigreed bowl. Thickly sliced farmer's cheese was piled high atop a plate adjacent to a cutting board covered in thick slices of rye bread; not the wimpy, pseudo-healthy bread of today's enlightened bakers, but the lard-laden, in-your-face, health-police rye that melted in your mouth without butter. But of course we slathered it in butter anyway, the kids falling over one another to be the first to cut the butt off the lamb butter (butter cast in a lamb-shaped mold). The only condiment allowed aside from salt and pepper was homemade horseradish, strong enough to clear the sinus passages of Rodin's "Thinker," and possibly change his name to Clueless. And before you ask about fruit and vegetables, there were none. Enough said. Dessert consisted of white and chocolate lamb cakes, along with bowls of pawed-over jellybeans.

But back to the men, who hovered around the table smoking cigars, drinking Cherry Kijafa, and feeling as if they could give Einstein's theory of relativity a run for its money. If they could only figure out who this Einstein guy was. For the uninitiated, Cherry Kijafa is a fortified fruit wine, possibly made in Denmark, with the unmistakable taste of cherry cough syrup and just a hint of motor oil lingering on the palate. How this became part of the tradition is beyond me, but my imagination drops me into a pre-children Easter meal, where the men discover to their horror that the Early Times bottle they were drinking from had a bottom. I envision my grandpa dispatching my dad to the medicine cabinet, and in years to come, not wanting to be found drinking cough medicine, they settle on the next best thing. Or maybe they just liked it.

Grandpa, as well as my aunts and uncle, are long gone. So are Mom and Dad, one brother, and a pair of cousins. I'm now the eldest of the family, which befuddles me to no end. Some of us still get together for Easter; the ones within driving distance and without commitments to in-laws or grown children. We've kept the same basic meal, although we have slipped in the occasional piece of fruit. I think back fondly to those days of cramped quarters and precarious food choices. I miss the billowing clouds of smoke from cigars and sausage grease and, in later years, the move up to the Cherry Kijafa table.

I miss sliding my polished penny loafers along plastic runners and shocking the snot out of my siblings. But mostly, I miss the family and the warm certainty that life would remain this way forever.

# Sister Abagail's Snow Socks

Thomas Wayne King
Solon Springs, WI

Sister Abagail darted swiftly through the packed, narrow lanes of new January snow. Duck Duck Goose was the game. Her kids couldn't catch her. The good sister's secret was her knee-high woolen socks: she wore them on the outside, over her other stockings. No boots. No shoes. Sister Abagail's thick, hand-knit socks gripped the dry snow firmly, giving her tremendous (seemingly divine) traction advantage over her young pupils. They loved it ... and her ... following their agile teacher in games of tag, Cut the Pie, Pom Pom Pullaway, Red Rover, and foot races around the churchyard. Sister Abagail, perhaps a decade older than her students, always won. Laughter and squeals of excitement set aglow this hardscrabble valley of northwestern Wisconsin in early 1917.

A timid, dark-haired boy, nine years old and always alone, walked past the lively group each day to and from his own rural, one-room public school just down the road.

Victor, in fourth grade, shared his school with kids of many ages and with their teacher, Miss Picotte. On his school hike each day, Victor noticed the activity at Sister Abagail's playground. Her winter exuberance with the schoolchildren was palpable, contagious. Just three months earlier, Victor and his mother, along with a few relatives, watched as his dad's casket was lowered into a cold, gaping November grave. Soon after, Vic's older, only brother left for the new war. Play and laughter had become rare in Victor's life.

It was a sunny late-January afternoon when Vic finally stopped on his way home to watch Sister Abagail's excited group. A dozen or so boys and girls about his age intently tried to break the chain of gripped hands in their enthusiastic playground game of Pom. Some of the kids looked familiar, and soon, the friendly, athletic sister ran over to him.

"Would you like to play?" she offered with her warm smile. "New snow is fun!"

Self-conscious and timid, Victor looked down at the snow and his rough-shod feet. He was poor.

"No, I can't today." Vic had on his only footwear other than his barn boots. The old lace-up, leather-soled shoes from his recently deceased father's closet were sadly, comically way too large, too slippery, too worn to walk in, let alone to play in with new kids. Embarrassed,

Victor explained that he was wearing ragged, dirty socks from his morning barn work, keeping them on because he rushed to get to school on time. His socks had big holes needing darning, and he didn't want the kids to see.

Sister Abagail kindly said she understood, and that he was welcome to stop by anytime. The sparkle in her eyes beckoned to Victor, along with the inviting gleam of bright snow. They bespoke a promise of fun and inclusion ... sometime. He walked home, thinking.

Several days later, as Vic did early morning farm chores, the powdery new snow was over his boots. His rural school seldom closed in winter, except during true blizzards because the twenty-some kids enrolled all lived on nearby farms. As durable, farm-strong children, they either hiked to school, rode on their families' horse-drawn sleighs and wagons, or slid quietly over the fields with their farmyard skis. Each winter school day was precious because family farm work often intruded on the kids' attendance during spring and fall months, when their help at home was essential.

Victor would rely on his simple, handmade skis. They had large leather toe straps, allowing him to wear barn boots and to move easily among farm outbuildings in deep snow. He just slipped the toes of his boots into the straps, and off he went for chores. That was how he would go to school today, skiing across fields over shorter routes than he could walk on roads. Vic knew his schoolhouse would be warm and welcoming, with a roaring wood fire that Miss Picotte built in the barrel stove. She and the older boys made certain their school was always cozy and safe for the smaller children.

Vic was excited. His mother had packed his lunch of two thick slices of homemade bread spread with lard, a small glass bottle she filled with milk from their one remaining cow, and a compact jar of maple syrup from their home sugar bush for dipping his bread.

When his school let out early that afternoon, Vic skied toward home, staying on snow-covered field trails that led to Sister Abagail's group. They were already out in the snow, playing and shouting. Even from a field away, Victor could hear the loud game of tag as the children and Sister sprinted and turned, twisted and dodged past one another to avoid becoming It. Laughter filled the valley.

As Vic skied up to the churchyard, he saw Sister Abagail running toward him in her black-and-white habit, with her distinctive wool outer socks gripping the sparkling snow. She was agile, quick, and sure-footed. And she was holding something in her hand. His heart soared.

"Hello, Victor! Would you like to play with us?" She knew his name.

Victor nodded. "Yes, I would. Thank you."

"Very well. Just place your skis and boots over there by the tree. Pull up your socks as tight as you can and tuck your pants in them. Then pull these big socks over the top of everything."

Sister Abagail handed him a new pair of gray bulky socks she had knit recently. Constructed from coarse, leftover rug yarn, they were rough, warm, and just what Vic needed to join the fun.

"They're yours, Victor." She spoke softly, so just he could hear.

Vic put on the socks and tried them out, marveling at how he could leap, run, stop ... and turn so fast. These were the best things he had ever worn on his feet. He joined with the kids and Sister Abagail as they lined up on two sides of the playground for Red Rover. Their second call was "Red Rover, Red Rover, let Victor come over!" Victor darted and dodged to the other side. In free! The bulky socks worked magically. So nimble. Such grip. Victor enjoyed a new warmth of acceptance, skill, and admiration.

For an hour that day, and on days to come, Vic found haven from sadness and poverty, an affirming refuge he could share; so different from what he had known over the past year. His father's death, his only brother's departure for war, and farm responsibilities, now Vic's and his mother's alone ... all of these faded in the glistening snow-globe world Sister Abagail and her students extended to him. Victor stopped by often to play during that exceptional winter.

Later in his life, Vic, my father, told me about the miracle of thick wool socks on cold, dry snow; the comfort and secure companionship he found with those kids; and, of course, dear Sister Abagail, his welcoming, rescuing angel. Victor believed she was truly heaven sent, just when he needed her. Sister Abagail's love of snow and fun changed Vic's life forever.

# When Madness Took Over the Milwaukee Repertory Theater

Ludmilla Bollow
Glendale, WI

The year was 1969.

The Milwaukee Repertory Theater was still housed in a small theater on Oakland Avenue, its last season there, before moving into the newly built Performing Arts Center. Their final show was The Persecution and Assassination of Jean-Paul Marat as Performed by the Inmates of the Asylum of Charenton under the Direction of the Marquis de Sade. The longest title, largest cast ever assembled by the Repertory.

It was a time of racial unrest in Milwaukee. Churning repercussions followed the open housing marches led by Father Groppi across bridges to the South. There were also various skirmishes, uprisings, and riots. Fear, anger, and bitterness were still turbulent among both blacks and whites.

Gene Lesser, the Repertory director, sought to capitalize on these festering emotions. "I'm looking for a general threat, an uneasiness over what 'might' happen" was his thrust for the play. "I'm seeking to shock by theater." And he succeeded.

Part of his strategy was to introduce black actors to Milwaukee audiences. For the lead role of Marat, he imported a nationally prominent black actor, Robert Jackson, the first black actor in the United States to play the role when Marat ran on Broadway in 1965. The nudity of Marat was a widely publicized highlight. Lesser promised no nudity and had Jackson sit or stand in a high tin bathtub throughout the performances.

The Oakland Avenue Theater, an intimate theater-in-the-round, was speedily transformed into an eighteenth-century lunatic asylum. The concrete block walls were painted stark white, then splattered layer upon layer with smudge and graffiti. Insane inmates were chained to these walls or sat on suspended crude plank shelves. Iron prison doors were installed at all the theater's entrances. Once the performance began, they were clanged shut menacingly. The ushers, athletic-looking men dressed as nuns of that century—rosaries, white winged caps—carried huge billy clubs, using them forcefully and frequently to subdue the inmates.

Before the audience was let in, the cast was already in place, performing their deranged sequences. Patrons walking through the iron gates into this strange asylum were suddenly lunged at by a half-clothed gigantic bearded black man, loosely held back by his rattling chains, sending many a matinee lady quickly back to the box office, and many times home.

It became the hottest ticket in town, sold out for its entire five-week run. During the six weeks of rehearsal and thirty-nine performances, I was one of the captive inmates performing in this tangled tale of literary madness.

Long before opening night, Lesser had been planning this unique theater explosion. He held acting classes earlier, promising roles to his students, "the opportunity to work with theater professionals." I was one of those eager students.

He also put out a call for local black actors, bringing in many who had never been on stage before. Miss Black Milwaukee was one of them. Another was a gentle male schoolteacher transformed into a fierce, raging maniac screaming blood-curdling cries. An older black lady, overweight and ailing, unable to follow stage rules but loving the whole experience, finally had her role curtailed to mostly sitting on a chair in an upper balcony.

It was a totally integrated cast. "Black is Beautiful" was proudly displayed on many T-shirts. The whites were called the "local locos." The inmate bit players ranged from the fragile elderly lady, who played strange squeaks on her violin during performances and fainted once during rehearsals, to the East Side lady, who placidly did needlework midst the backstage bedlam and held a grand opening night party at her elegant mansion.

My role? I sat on a wooden wall shelf, crying and whimpering while cradling my crude straw doll. Next to me, chained to the wall, was a young man foaming at the mouth making strange guttural sounds. One night, he told me not to worry if he passed out, as he had epilepsy. Well, he did have scenes where he was beaten and had to pass out. So, I was never sure if it was acting or for real.

The more experienced actors, and a special group of singers/dancers/clowns/jugglers, were in the higher echelon. The stars—Erika Slezak, William McKeregan, and Michael Fairman—were well known and well cast.

We were all aware of our designated differences. Non-stars were the inmates who had the small cramped dressing room at the front of the theater. Upper level actors had the real dressing rooms upstairs. We were segregated by roles, not by race.

There was a desperate shortage of bathrooms for this cast of forty-two-plus. We were told there wasn't time for us to access restrooms between acts. It was more important for the leads to be able to use them. "Go before the show," we were warned.

At the end of the first act, the cast paraded around in the theater in a long, tedious procession. We wore thick masks, heavy robes, carrying lighted candles and perspiring heavily. We locos had to then continue marching out the backdoor into the cold alley to get back to our tiny dressing room at the front of the theater. We were told, "There is no room for you to hang around backstage." We protested this during rehearsals, but the fierce production manager was adamant. "Background people have no right to clutter up the backstage."

We started moaning collectively, protesting the need for full makeup and costumes during rehearsals while the "stars" remained in their street apparel. The stress of being insane inmates steadily intensified our outbursts about our poor, uncaring treatment.

It was during one of the hell-week rehearsals that "our champion," Robert Jackson, suddenly got up from his bathtub, interrupting the director's notes, giving one of his most memorable speeches in his beautiful, eloquent, and commanding voice.

"I know firsthand about prejudice, segregation, and how it was used to keep people down," he cried out. "I am tired of the local actors being treated like second-class citizens! We are all equal!" he screamed. "This is what this whole play is about—equality!" He continued on that he wanted equality to extend beyond the play into the treatment of the cast, if the message was worth anything at all. "I am not going to put up with it anymore!"

Grateful applause erupted from all of us. Finally, someone made us feel we were more than piles of dirty rags and insane décor on the walls and floors.

After that resounding reprimand, room was made for us backstage.

# Whenever Women Have Lived

Lisa Rivero
Milwaukee, WI


This girl is familiar. A visitor. The fat woman in the white belted dress had walked into her room in her solid monochrome way and said, "You have a visitor," just like that, cheerful and certain, as if visitors arrive every day. The fat woman is the same woman who wakes her and helps her out of bed and bathes her and smooths her sheets and places a drop of too-sweet perfume on her pillow on Sundays. She is familiar, too, but in a different way, a favorite, crumbly, store-bought cookie that tastes the same every time.

The girl sits on a folding chair and is pretty as only the young can be pretty, arms and legs as smooth as cream-colored lake stones, hairless and firm. The girl is talking. "I'm here. What do you want me to say? I know. I'm trying, but it's just so, you know, depressing." While she talks, her free hand gestures to various parts of the room and back, tucks her hair behind her ear, smooths the hem of her blouse, rubs her knee, never stops moving. Her other hand holds a phone to her ear. How small the phone is! So tiny and black. When did phones get so small? Something about the girl's eyes, big round eyes the color of maple syrup, something about the way they grow rounder when she talks instead of narrowing makes her think of something else, someone else, but the thought is unfixed, already changing; bubbles that race to the surface only to disappear in a lemon mist. Martin would know this girl. He never forgets a name or a face. She would ask Martin. "Mom, she doesn't even know who I am."

Her eyes move from the girl to the open window, where a yellow bird looks in from the low-hanging branch of a willow tree, its smooth head tilted to one side. The dip in the road behind the barn is lined with willows. Their sleepy branches fall heavily to meet the ground, and she and her cousin play in the coolness of the willow canopies when the Nebraska wind blows hot and dry. They sit with their legs crossed and eat mulberries and wild cherries with red-stained fingers until their stomachs ache. The wind through this window is a different kind of hot—heavy, wet, pregnant. That other old wind is as dry and light as the summer dust she sweeps off the front steps every morning after breakfast. Martin would know who this girl is. The thought comforts her.

The visitor is now standing up, leaning over to kiss her cheek. But she doesn't know this girl whose hair smells of lilacs, of the first breath of purple spring air. She smiles and knots her hand around smooth, slender fingers and squeezes. Then the girl is gone, but the lilacs remain. These flowers grow wherever women have lived. That's what Mamma always said. Not lilacs but another purple flower. The tall purple flowers grow everywhere alongside roads and in ditches and at the edge of fields. She'll pick them to give to Mamma who will place them precisely in the light blue glass vase that sets always on the white countertop next to the kitchen sink. She will show them to the baby. Her hands move to her belly, swollen with memory. The baby will be a girl. Of this she is certain.

## Music and the Man

Susan Hunnicutt
Milwaukee, WI


You took the music with you
When you left
I didn't know

That silence could be deafening
Quiet screams hello

No fingers touch the keyboard
Strum or pick guitar
The tunes no longer linger
In the house, they've gone so far

You took the music with you
When you left
I didn't know

That I might learn in measured time
To let peace in, the soul will grow

If we are meant to be apart
May solace be our separate songs
But if we stay together
New harmony belongs

You took the music with you
When you left
I didn't know

# On Valentine's Eve

Lisa Vihos
Sheboygan, WI

How long before this little piece of ecstasy will melt away?
How to keep this fragile sweet from being devoured by
the gravity of my heart? Our time together, a piece
of chocolate on my tongue, going faster than I
had intended. I thought we might hang on
but every day, we are smaller and smaller,
like that scrap of soap I keep using
in the shower, or the orange moon,
hanging low on the horizon.

When we are far from the lake,
the moon looks huge. But as we approach the bluff,
the moon becomes reduced. Contrary to logic,
the closer we get to a thing, the smaller it
becomes. With proximity, all things
lose their meaning. Moons, loves,
dreams stay large only when
they remain distant.
Close up, too much
warmth, too much
familiarity.

Close up, things shrivel, shrink,
and melt away, like tongued-
chocolate, leaving only an
after-taste, returned to
the nothingness
from which
it came.

# Friendship by the Slice

Nancy Runner
Weston, WI

Mildred and Trudy, who lived in the same senior apartment building, seemed to have little in common, yet they did everything together. The other residents called them "the odd couple." They were both in that 70-90 hard-to-tell-your-exact-age phase of life. Trudy was the short, round one with a ready smile, who never complained about her poor eyesight. Mildred was tall and thin, with a rusty-colored perm and a tight-lipped smile. Trudy wore comfortable sweats, while Mildred preferred slacks with sweaters. Mildred called herself "practical," but she veered into the bitter as when she was overheard to complain, "I moved here to be close to my kids, but I never see them." Trudy was the generous one, always taking coffee and a treat to the ladies in the retirement community beauty shop.

Mildred often took Trudy grocery shopping since Trudy had been forced to give up driving. As Trudy explained with a laugh, "The police are funny about people going over that yellow line." On their most recent weekly shopping trip Trudy picked up some chicken for dinner, potatoes, and the first green beans that looked any good that spring.

Then Trudy saw cherry pies were on sale. "I think I'll get two," she said.

"What do you need two for?" Mildred huffed.

"I can freeze one," said Trudy. "You never know when you might need a nice cherry pie. And these look good."

At the checkout, Trudy dug in her handbag for her ancient coin purse. She counted the bills and coins, but found she was a couple dollars short.

Mildred pulled her cart next to Trudy's and plopped her big, brown purse on the conveyor belt.

She pawed in it until she found her wallet. Then Mildred handed Trudy the dollars she needed.

Around 6:00 p.m., after her supper, Mildred sat down with the newspaper. She soon put it aside and looked for something on TV, but couldn't find anything she wanted to watch. She picked up her knitting but quit after two rows. She decided to wander over to Trudy's apartment. Trudy was just cutting herself a piece of cherry pie and offered one to Mildred. They sat out on the apartment balcony and enjoyed the mild evening, savoring the sweetness mixed with tart cherries. Trudy served coffee, too.

They reminisced about their grandmothers' cooking methods. Both agreed their grandmothers didn't really use cookbooks but followed the old-time measurements of a "pinch" of this or a "handful" of that. Mildred smiled as she remembered, "My grandmother used to say, 'add butter the size of an egg.'"

Trudy perked up. "That's interesting. I never heard of anyone buttering the sides of an egg. Why would she do that?"

Mildred put her coffee mug down and looked at Trudy in disbelief. "I didn't say 'butter the sides of an egg.' That's ridiculous. You didn't hear me correctly. Are you wearing your hearing aid? I said grandma would add butter the SIZE of an egg!"

"Oh," chuckled Trudy. "That makes more sense."

After about an hour, Mildred stood to go back to her own apartment. "Don't forget those two dollars you owe me," she reminded Trudy.

"Well, you ate a piece of the cherry pie," Trudy answered, blinking behind her thick glasses.

"That was out of the first pie not the second one I lent you the money for. Besides, it was a small piece."

"I'll pay you next time I go to the bank."

Mildred knew that could be a while. "Just give me a piece of that pie to take home and we'll call it even."

Trudy cut Mildred a good-sized slice and slid it onto a pretty china plate with a platinum rim. She covered it with a red cotton napkin and handed it to her friend. It was good to have a friend who would drive you to the grocery store and hand you money in a tight spot. Mildred accepted the pie. It was good to have a friend whose apartment you could visit when you felt a little lonely….a friend with an extra cherry pie in the freezer.

"See you tomorrow," they both said.

Many, many thanks to the WWA members who
contributed to our first
Creative Wisconsin
Literary Journal

For more information about the
Wisconsin Writers Association, please visit our
website at: www.wiwrite.org

Made in the USA
Lexington, KY
20 September 2017